SPORTS ENCYCLOPEDIAS

THE WORLD SOCCER ENCYCLOPEDIA

BY BRENDAN FLYNN

Encyclopedias

An Imprint of Abdo Reference

abdobooks.com

TABLE OF CONTENTS

HISTORY

Soccer is known for engaging rivalries and showdowns between star players, such as Lionel Messi, *middle*, and Kylian Mbappé, *right*.

THE WORLD OF SOCCER

Soccer is widely considered the world's most popular sport. An estimated 250 million players in more than 200 countries play the sport. Meanwhile, some 3.5 billion people consider themselves soccer fans.

Every year, professional soccer leagues around the globe showcase the amazing skills of their players. The best players represent their countries by playing for national teams. Every four years, the top men's and women's national teams compete in their respective World Cups. These are the most prestigious soccer tournaments in the world. In addition, soccer continues to thrive at the youth level.

EARLY HISTORY

People have been playing soccer-like games for much of recorded history. More than 3,000 years ago, ancient cultures in Central and South America played some of the earliest-known games involving a ball. The Aztec people in present-day Mexico called their version of the game *tlachtli*.

The first-known game that involved kicking a ball was *cuju*. People in China played it as far back as 300 BCE. From *kemari* in Japan to *marn grook* in Australia, numerous ancient games could be considered early versions of soccer.

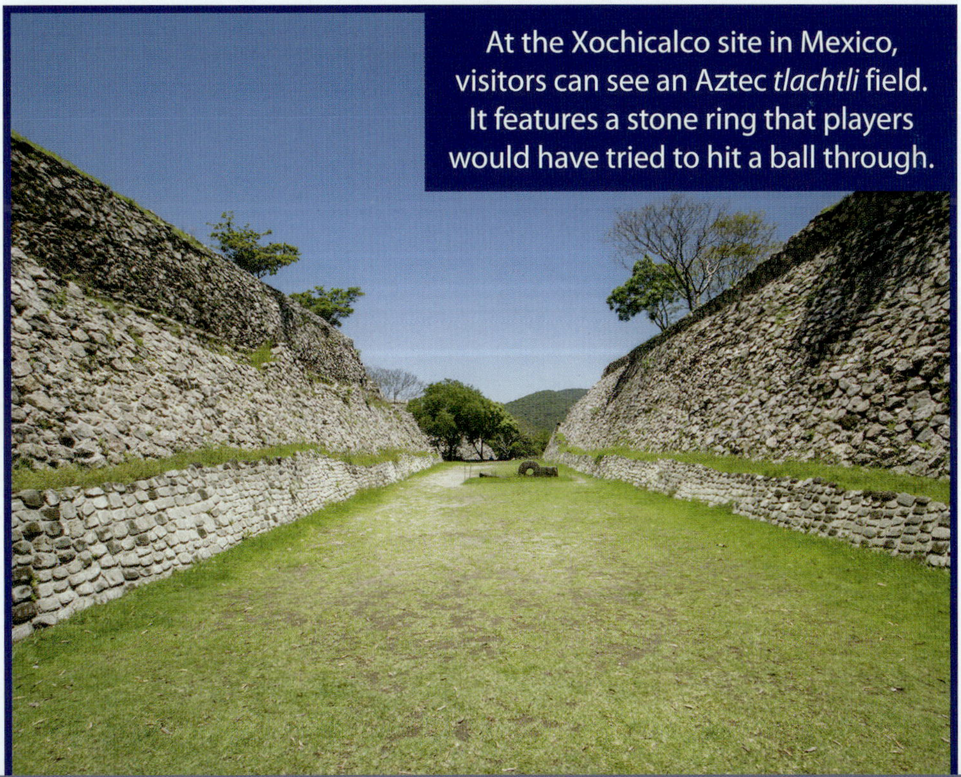

At the Xochicalco site in Mexico, visitors can see an Aztec *tlachtli* field. It features a stone ring that players would have tried to hit a ball through.

SOCCER ORIGINS

In the 1100s CE, a game called folkball emerged in England. It was similar to soccer. But one big difference was that folkball players could punch the ball and tackle each other. Eventually, folkball was banned for being too violent.

A safer form of the game became popular in the 1800s. It was generally known as football. People played it at English public schools. But each school had its own rules for the game. Some schools allowed players to pick up and carry the ball. Others didn't.

Early versions of soccer in England had varying rules, such as allowing players to use their hands.

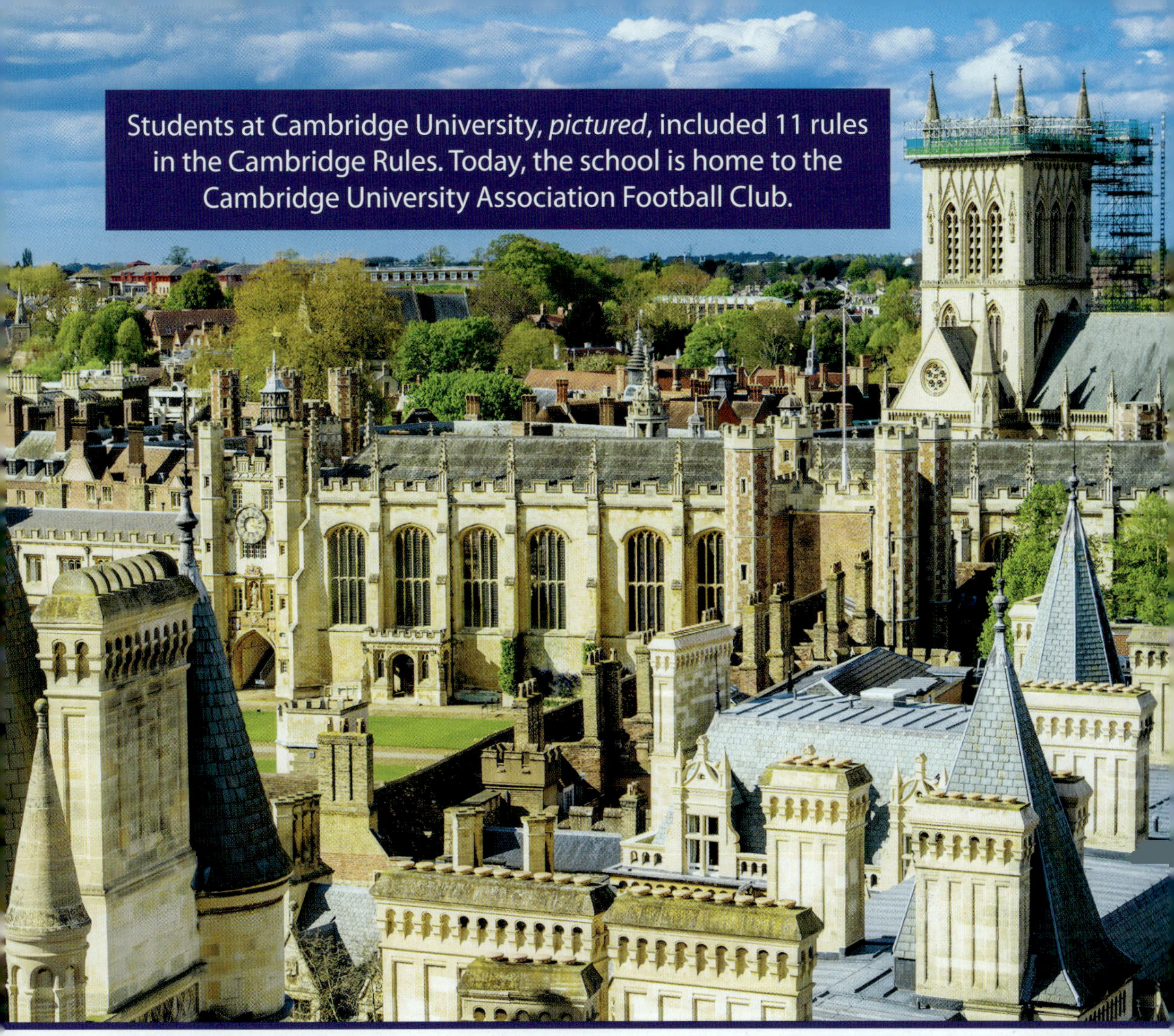

Students at Cambridge University, *pictured*, included 11 rules in the Cambridge Rules. Today, the school is home to the Cambridge University Association Football Club.

To standardize the competition, a group of students from Cambridge University wrote a set of rules in 1848. The so-called Cambridge Rules were nailed to trees at local parks so people could learn them. The Cambridge Rules established many basic guidelines that are still in place today. They were adopted by the Football Association (FA) of England in 1863. The rules spread around the world, thanks to an increase in global travel. Soon, people all over the planet were playing the same game, governed by the same set of rules.

The Sheffield Football Club was founded by Nathaniel Creswick and William Prest. Members of the club developed their own set of rules in 1858.

THE FIRST CLUBS

As soccer became more organized, players joined clubs to form teams. Clubs often centered around graduates from different schools. The earliest-known school-based club was formed in Sheffield, England, in 1855.

Other soccer clubs were sponsored by local businesses. Some factories started clubs so their workers could play together. Eventually, these types of teams became more common than school clubs. Business-based clubs had unique advantages. Businesses could hire the best players to work at their factories or stores. Then they could add those players to

THE NAME *SOCCER*

English people played two types of football. One allowed players to pick up the ball. This version of the game became known as rugby. The other type was played with only the feet. This game was called association football. Before long, "association" was shortened to "soccer."

their soccer teams. This was the start of pro soccer in England.

The popularity of club soccer helped the game spread throughout the United Kingdom. Soon clubs sprang up in Ireland, Scotland, and Wales. This was just the beginning of the sport's growth.

Popular British team Manchester United began as Newton Heath, the club of employees from the Lancashire and Yorkshire Railway. In 1885, Sam Black was photographed wearing the team uniform.

EARLY CUPS AND LEAGUES

As competition between soccer clubs heated up, people organized tournaments to determine which club was the best. The FA Cup is the oldest soccer tournament. It began in 1871. It has been held every year since, except for a few times. After the 1914–15 Cup, the competition was canceled until 1919 due to World War I (1914–1918). It was canceled again after 1938–39 because of World War II (1939–1945). The Cup resumed in 1945.

Open to both professional and amateur English men's teams, the tournament regularly draws more than 700 teams.

After winning the first FA Cup in 1871–72, each member of the Wanderers received a gold medal. There is only one known surviving winner's medal from that year.

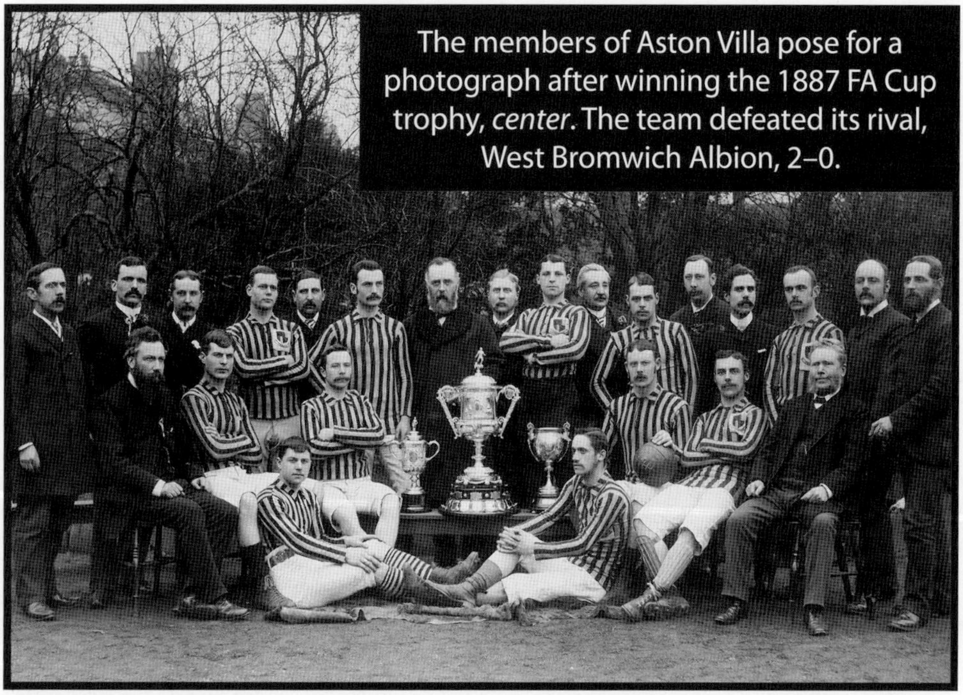

The members of Aston Villa pose for a photograph after winning the 1887 FA Cup trophy, *center*. The team defeated its rival, West Bromwich Albion, 2–0.

The first FA Cup champions were the Wanderers, a team founded by former students from the Harrow School in London, England. True to its name, the team didn't have a home stadium. The Wanderers became one of the first major soccer clubs in England.

The FA Cup grew quickly. Only 12 teams competed in 1871. By 1879, that number had jumped to 50 teams. Soon, the clubs started selling tickets to fans. Then, in 1888, the English Football League (EFL) was formed to help organize England's soccer leagues. Twelve clubs joined the organization that year. Preston North End was the first Football League champion. Over time, more clubs joined the organization. The Football League established multiple divisions.

A GLOBAL GAME

Club soccer wasn't the only version of the game. Countries also formed national teams. These teams featured a country's best players.

The first international match took place on November 30, 1872, in Glasgow, Scotland. Teams representing England and Scotland competed against each other. All the Scottish players came from the local Queen's Park club. The English team was composed of players from nine FA clubs. The match ended in a scoreless draw.

The first international soccer match, which featured Scotland and England, took place at the West of Scotland Cricket Club. William Ralston illustrated scenes from the match.

It wasn't long before soccer's popularity spread beyond the British Isles. At the time, the British Empire extended throughout the world. The country had colonies in regions such as Africa, Central America, and South America. British soldiers and citizens lived in and traveled to these colonies. They brought their favorite sport with them.

Soccer took root in continental Europe in the 1870s. Clubs sprang up in the Netherlands, Belgium, Switzerland, and Denmark. Eventually, leagues formed in Italy, Spain, Germany, and France. Over the next century, these four countries would join England as hotbeds of the sport.

German teachers August Hermann and Konrad Koch first learned about soccer in England. They introduced the sport to Germany around 1874.

SOCCER IN SOUTH AMERICA

After soccer became popular in Europe, it quickly spread across the ocean. British sailors introduced the sport to people in South America. The first South American soccer club was formed in Buenos Aires, Argentina, in 1867. Around that time, British railway workers formed another club in Rosario, Argentina.

The first Argentinian league soccer championship took place in 1893. At the time, the sport was mostly played by British citizens living abroad. Similar patterns emerged in

The first-known soccer match in Argentina took place at Buenos Aires Cricket Club in 1867.

Scottish teacher Alexander Watson Hutton is credited with establishing the Argentine Association Football League in 1893. He is sometimes called the "Father of Argentine Football."

other countries. British workers formed clubs and leagues in Brazil, Uruguay, Colombia, Chile, Venezuela, and Paraguay.

Eventually, South Americans began to embrace soccer. It became especially popular with working-class boys and men. They could play forms of the game in their free time in the street or on vacant fields. Soccer soon became part of the cultural identity of many South American countries.

FIFA was originally headquartered in Amsterdam, the Netherlands. In 1932, its headquarters moved to Zurich, Switzerland.

FORMATION OF FIFA

By the early 1900s, so many countries had formed national soccer teams that some people began calling for an organization to oversee the sport. On May 21, 1904, the Fédération Internationale de Football Association (FIFA) was founded in Paris, France. Seven countries—Belgium, Denmark, France, the Netherlands, Spain, Sweden, and Switzerland—were counted as founding members. England and Germany soon joined the organization, too. It wasn't much longer before FIFA's reach spanned the globe, with South Africa, the United States, Canada, and Argentina joining the group.

FIFA's goal was to promote soccer and "foster friendly relations" between members of competing nations. It also helped oversee rule changes and arranged international matches. Soccer had become an official Olympic sport in 1900, and FIFA became involved with Olympic soccer in 1908.

But FIFA's biggest contribution to the sport is the World Cup. This men's competition was first held in 1930, and it soon became one of the world's most popular sports tournaments. The Women's World Cup was first played in 1991. Today, 211 national associations are FIFA members. National associations are organizations that govern soccer in a country or region.

Uruguay's José Nasazzi, *second from left*, shakes hands with Argentina's Manuel "Nolo" Ferreira, *second from right*, before the 1930 World Cup final. The two players served as team captains.

CLUB COMPETITION HEATS UP

The World Cup gave national teams a chance to compete against one another. But club soccer has long been organized locally. Typically, each country had its own domestic league. But there was no way to determine a global club champion. The first attempt to settle the argument on the field came in 1951. The Copa Rio de Janeiro, or Copa Rio, featured eight men's league champion clubs. Two were from Brazil, one was from Uruguay, and five were from Europe.

In the final of the 1951 Copa Rio, Brazilian team Palmeiras, *pictured*, faced off against Italian team Juventus.

Members of Real Madrid celebrate their victory over Stade de Reims in the 1956 European Cup. The event took place at the Parc des Princes stadium in Paris, France.

Soon, competitions sprang up on different continents, pitting clubs from the same member associations against one another. The first European Cup took place in 1955–56. The champions of 16 European domestic leagues were invited. The final match took place in Paris, where Real Madrid of Spain defeated Stade de Reims of France by a score of 4–3.

The 1956 victory was the first of five consecutive European Cup titles for Real Madrid. Other European teams emerged as powerhouses in the 1960s and 1970s as the professional game began to thrive in Europe. These included Bayern Munich of Germany, Liverpool of England, AC Milan of Italy, and Ajax of the Netherlands.

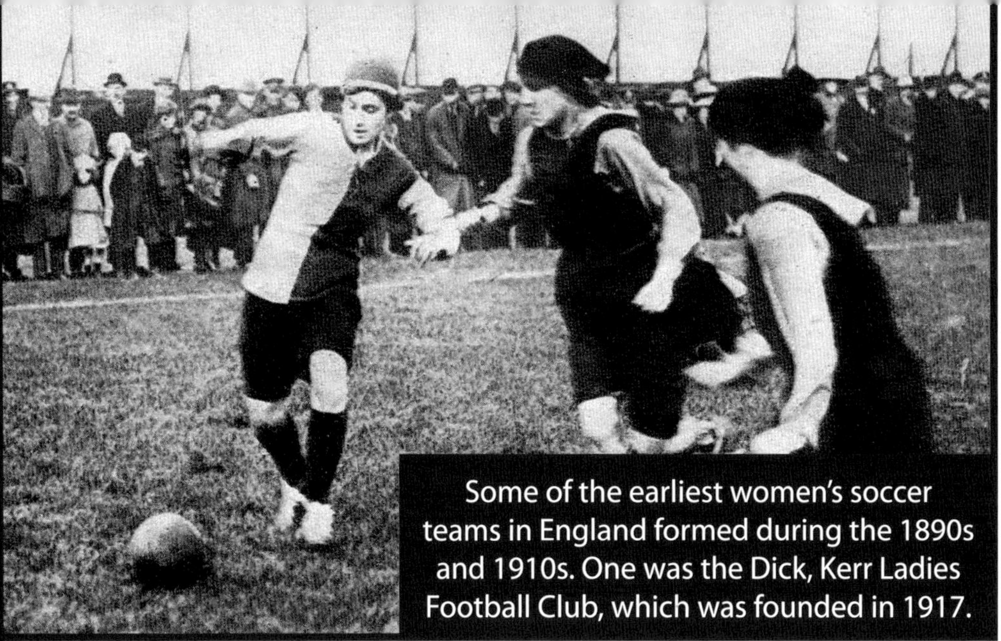

Some of the earliest women's soccer teams in England formed during the 1890s and 1910s. One was the Dick, Kerr Ladies Football Club, which was founded in 1917.

WOMEN'S SOCCER EMERGES

Women have been playing soccer for as long as men have. The British Ladies Football Club formed in 1894. It was the first professional women's soccer club. The team was met with resistance from men, who weren't used to sharing the field with women. But female soccer players persevered and even thrived. When thousands of men left the United Kingdom to fight in World War I, women took their places in factories and formed their own soccer teams.

Women's soccer became so popular that men returning from war saw it as a threat. Many people thought soccer was a men's sport, and they didn't want to share fields or potential earnings with female players. Because of this, the FA wanted to limit women's ability to play soccer. It couldn't make women's soccer illegal. So it banned FA clubs from allowing women to play in their stadiums.

The ban put the brakes on women's soccer for half a century. But in the 1970s, the tide began to turn. An unofficial women's world championship was held in Italy in 1970. Two years later, the US government passed Title IX, a law requiring gender equity in public institutions, such as schools. This law led to more girls and women playing soccer. The US Women's National Team (USWNT) formed in 1985, and the first FIFA-sanctioned Women's World Cup took place in 1991. The USWNT won the event.

Englishwoman Lily Parr, *second from left*, became a star player for the Dick, Kerr Ladies Football Club in the mid-1900s. She was known for her powerful kicks and helped increase interest in women's soccer.

PREMIER LEAGUE AND CHAMPIONS LEAGUE

In 1992, two changes altered the face of soccer in Europe and beyond. First, the European Cup got a new name and new look. It became the UEFA Champions League. This name recognized the governing body of European soccer, the Union of European Football Associations.

The tournament adopted a new model that followed the World Cup. In this model, qualifying clubs from around Europe were placed into four-team groups. Each team in a group played its fellow members twice. Group winners competed in the final. Later, UEFA added more teams and knockout stages, which helped increase the drama and popularity of the sport.

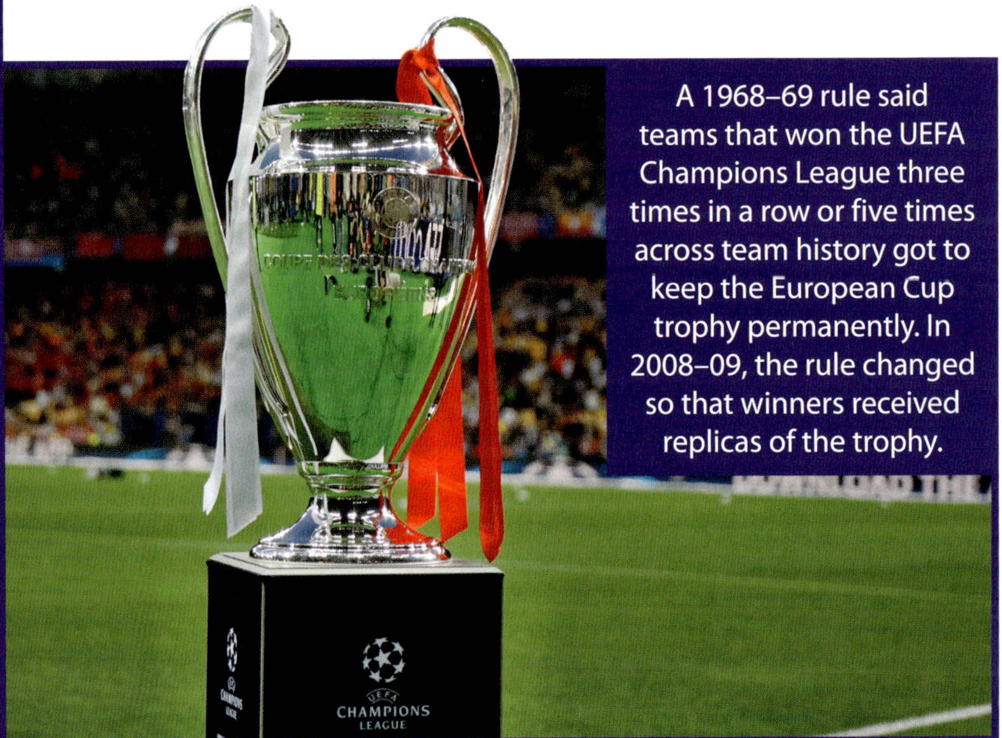

A 1968–69 rule said teams that won the UEFA Champions League three times in a row or five times across team history got to keep the European Cup trophy permanently. In 2008–09, the rule changed so that winners received replicas of the trophy.

Alex Ferguson was manager of Manchester United when the team became the first Premier League champion in May 1993.

That same year, English soccer went through a major reorganization. The top 22 men's clubs split away from the EFL to form the Premier League. A variety of factors went into this decision, including TV broadcast rights, profit sharing, and stadium issues. Because clubs gained more control over themselves, they could also make more money. The new league was wildly popular. It helped spike interest in English club soccer throughout the world.

In 2022, the men's World Cup took place in Qatar. In the final, Argentina and France faced off at Lusail Stadium.

MEN'S SOCCER TODAY

Men's soccer has continued to thrive. It is still one of the most popular sports in the world. The World Cup is the sport's top competition. European and South American countries won every World Cup through 2022. But with each edition, different groups of teams contend for championships. Beginning in 2002, World Cup champions came from six different countries—Brazil, Italy, Spain, Germany, France, and Argentina.

On the club side, countries continue to have their own leagues. Europe, North America, South America, Africa, Asia, and Oceania each have continental championships as well. The UEFA Champions League is considered the highest level of

club soccer. However, an expanded Club World Cup set to debut in 2025 could change that.

Professional soccer has also become more entrenched in North America. In the wake of the 1994 World Cup, which was hosted by the United States, Major League Soccer (MLS) began play in 1996. The quality of play has improved, and the league has expanded rapidly after starting with only ten clubs. In 2023, St. Louis City SC became the twenty-ninth member of MLS. San Diego was scheduled to become the thirtieth member in 2025.

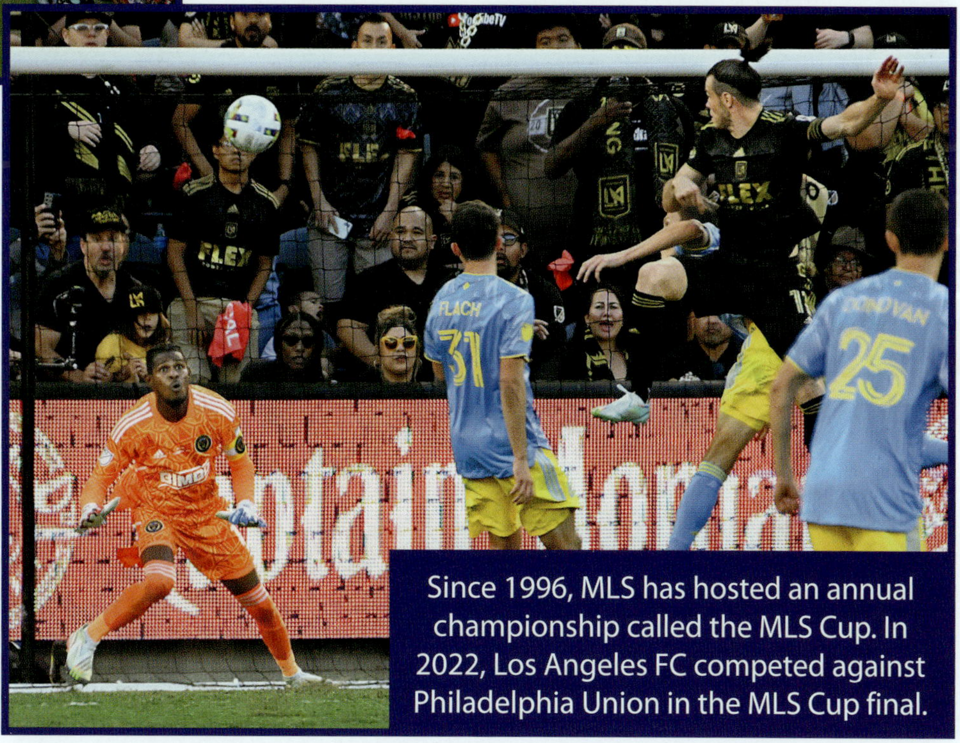

Since 1996, MLS has hosted an annual championship called the MLS Cup. In 2022, Los Angeles FC competed against Philadelphia Union in the MLS Cup final.

WOMEN'S SOCCER TODAY

Women's soccer has grown at an impressive rate. The Women's World Cup was once viewed as little more than a curiosity. But then the United States hosted the tournament in 1999. The USWNT won a thrilling final. The team defeated China in a shoot-out in front of a sold-out crowd in Southern California. The event's success showed TV executives that there was an appetite for women's soccer, especially among American audiences.

Two attempts at establishing a women's pro league in the United States were quickly abandoned due to a lack

USWNT members Brandi Chastain, Julie Foudy, and Carla Overbeck, *left to right*, celebrate after winning the 1999 Women's World Cup.

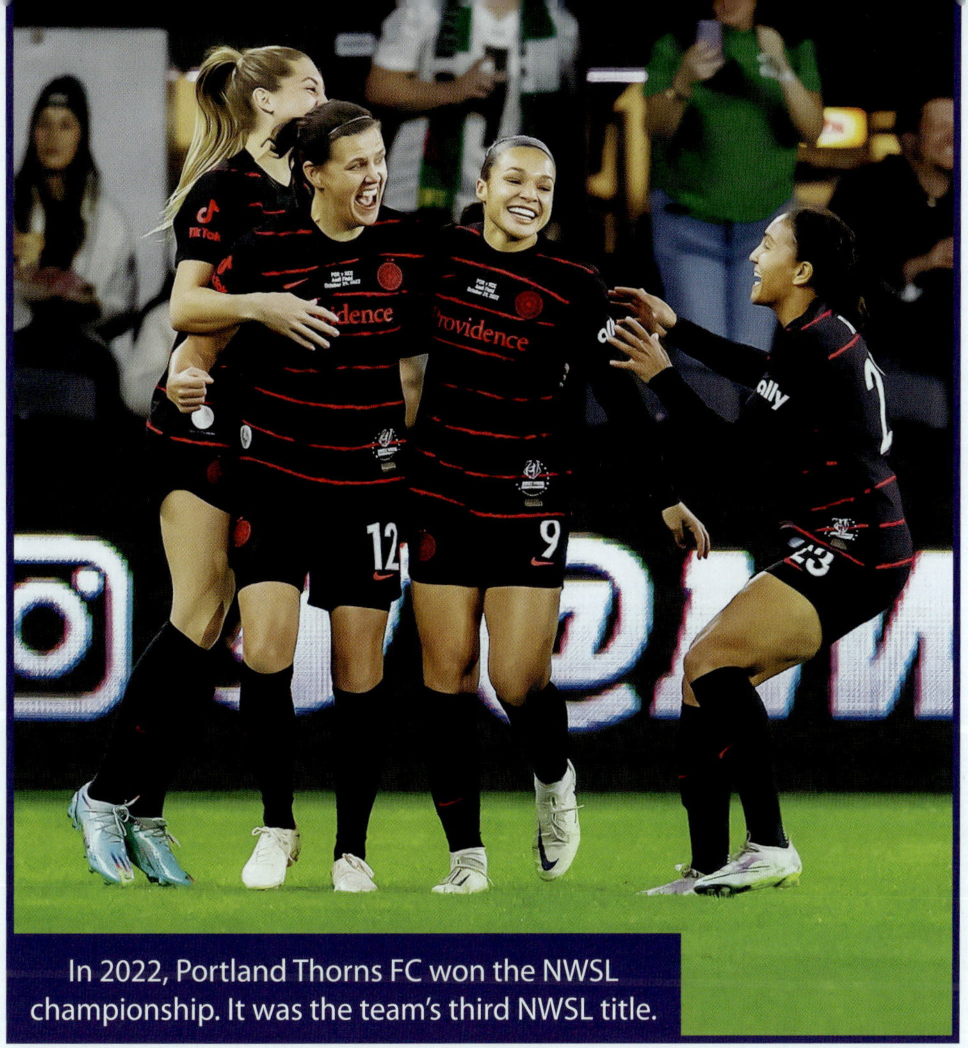

In 2022, Portland Thorns FC won the NWSL championship. It was the team's third NWSL title.

of money. But in 2012, the National Women's Soccer League (NWSL) began. As of 2024, the league has grown from eight to 14 teams. It has also landed a national TV contract.

Women's club soccer has also become more popular in Europe, where many of the traditional men's organizations have started women's teams. Some of the world's top female players can be found on the rosters of Arsenal, Chelsea, Barcelona, Lyon, and Wolfsburg. The UEFA Women's European Championship and Women's Champions League have also grown over the years.

COMPETITIONS AND LEAGUES

CLUB VS. COUNTRY

Top-level soccer is divided into two types of competition: club and country. Club soccer is professional. Players sign contracts to play for their club for a set period. They are often paid well. Club teams play most games against teams from other clubs in their own countries. But there are also international club competitions.

Many club teams have large fan bases. Two popular English clubs are Liverpool, *red*, and Manchester City, *blue*.

The best players have a chance to play for their national teams, which represent an entire country. Players can compete for the country in which they were born. National teams face off in continent-wide tournaments. Every four years, the best teams compete in the World Cup or Women's World Cup. These are usually held during international breaks, during which professional leagues suspend their schedules. This allows players to train and join their national teams for tournaments.

SOCCER POSITIONS

Soccer teams consist of 11 players. One player serves as goalkeeper, or goalie. They defend their team's net and keep opponents from scoring. The other ten members are outfield players. They include defenders, midfielders, and forwards. These players pass the ball to teammates, defend their team's net, or score goals.

Australian Tameka Yallop, *left*, and Brazilian Formiga, *right*, compete for their national teams in the 2019 Women's World Cup.

MEN'S WORLD CUP

By the 1920s, many men's soccer players had turned professional. Clubs paid them to play. Soon, people called for an international tournament to determine which country had the best players.

In 1928, FIFA announced plans for the first World Cup. Uruguay would be the host country. The tournament featured 13 national teams. It took place during an economic depression in Europe, which prevented many European countries from participating.

The World Cup took place from July 13 to July 30, 1930. About 90,000 fans watched the final. Uruguay defeated

Uruguay scores a goal during the first men's World Cup final in 1930. The tournament took place in Montevideo, the capital of Uruguay.

Members of Uruguay's national team pose for a photo during the 1930 World Cup final. The full squad included 22 players.

Argentina 4–2, becoming the first World Cup champions. The tournament was a success. Since then, the World Cup has been held every four years, except for 1942 and 1946, when it was canceled due to World War II.

To participate in the tournament, teams must qualify for it. The host country automatically qualifies. The qualifying process, structure, and schedule have changed over the years and were set to change again in 2026. In 2026, the number of teams will expand from 32 to 48. These will be divided into 12 groups of four. Teams will play against others in their group. The top two teams from each group, along with the eight best third-place teams, will move to knockout stages. Teams will advance through knockout stages until reaching a final two.

During the 1934 World Cup, Vittorio Pozzo, *left*, served as coach and manager of the Italian national team.

THE 1930s

Italy hosted the second World Cup in 1934. Uruguay, the defending champions, were not among the 16 participants. Uruguay chose not to participate because it was upset that so many European teams had not participated in the 1930 event. The 1934 tournament was notable because FIFA introduced a knockout format, which involved single elimination for four rounds. In the final, Italian Angelo Schiavio's stoppage-time goal helped Italy beat Czechoslovakia 2–1.

In 1938, France hosted the World Cup. But global politics cast a shadow over the event. Argentina joined Uruguay in boycotting the World Cup. The country was upset that the tournament had not returned to South America. Meanwhile, world politics were simmering, and war was brewing in Europe. These issues prevented several countries from participating. Italy survived the 16-team bracket to win its second straight World Cup, defeating Hungary 4–2 in the final.

Italian Giuseppe Meazza, *left*, and Hungarian György Sárosi, *right*, shake hands before the 1938 World Cup final in Paris. The two players served as team captains.

THE 1950s

The next two World Cup cycles were canceled due to World War II. The tournament resumed in 1950. Since Europe was recovering from the war, the World Cup returned to South America. Brazil hosted, and matches took place at Rio de Janeiro's Maracanã Stadium. Transatlantic flight made it easier for European teams to travel to South America and participate. Group play returned to the Cup, too. Uruguay won its second World Cup in its second appearance at the tournament. It defeated Brazil in front of nearly 200,000 fans.

Maracanã Stadium was built to be used for the 1950 World Cup. At the time of its completion, it could hold about 200,000 fans. Today, it is the largest stadium in Brazil.

West German team members Fritz Walter, *top center*, and Horst Eckel, *top right*, celebrate after winning the 1954 World Cup final in Bern, Switzerland. Their victory became known as the "Miracle of Bern."

In 1954, Switzerland hosted the World Cup. Hungary entered as the favorite, thanks to its star striker Ferenc Puskás. But the Hungarians were shocked by West Germany's team, a first-time participant. After falling behind in the final, West Germany rallied for a 3–2 victory.

Sweden hosted the 1958 World Cup. That year, Uruguay failed to qualify. But South America was still well represented, with Brazilian stars Garrincha and Pelé showing their skills on the world stage for the first time. France's Just Fontaine scored 13 goals, a record no player has matched since. But 17-year-old Pelé stole the show. He scored six goals, including two in the final, leading Brazil to victory over Sweden.

Soccer stars Garrincha, Didi, Pelé, Vavá, and Zagallo, *left to right*, were all part of Brazil's national team during the 1962 World Cup.

THE 1960s

Political instability in Argentina led FIFA to set the 1962 tournament in Chile. The Chileans scored a big upset when they beat the Soviet Union, which had won the first European Championship two years earlier. The World Cup was marred by violent gameplay, including a brawl between Chile and Italy in a first-round match. Pelé, considered the world's best player, was injured in Brazil's second match. His team had to continue playing without him. But Brazil went on to defeat Chile in the semifinals. In the final, it beat Czechoslovakia 3–1, claiming its second straight World Cup title.

In 1966, the World Cup was held in England for the first time. The tournament featured many memorable moments, such as Italy getting eliminated by North Korea. Pelé limped through another tournament and vowed to retire from international play after suffering more rough treatment on the field. But the 1966 World Cup is best remembered for a controversial goal awarded to England's Geoff Hurst in extra time of the final. It proved to be the game winner, with England defeating West Germany 4–2.

England's George Cohen, *left*, and Martin Peters, *center*, face off against West Germany's Lothar Emmerich, *right*, during the 1966 World Cup final. The match took place at Wembley Stadium in London.

THE 1970s

Mexico hosted the 1970 World Cup, bringing the tournament to North American soil for the first time. Its team reached the knockout rounds before losing to Italy. West Germany got revenge on England in an extra-time match, defeating the defending champs in the quarterfinals.

The tournament was famous for a photo of Brazil's players carrying Pelé off the field. It was Pelé's final World Cup, and he went out in style. Pelé scored four goals, including one in the final. Brazil won its third World Cup with a 4–1 victory over Italy.

Pelé, *center*, is lifted into the air by teammates after winning the 1970 World Cup final.

Franz Beckenbauer holds the World Cup trophy after leading West Germany to victory in 1974. Beckenbauer served as team captain during the tournament.

West Germany hosted the 1974 World Cup. The top three finishers came from Europe. Poland nabbed a third-place win over Brazil. The final was a showdown among three of the world's best players: Gerd Müller, Franz Beckenbauer, and Johan Cruyff. Müller and Beckenbauer led West Germany to victory, defeating Cruyff and the Netherlands.

The World Cup returned to Argentina in 1978. The country had not yet won a World Cup. Argentina used a 6–0 win over Peru to reach the final. Then it scored two extra-time goals to beat the Netherlands 3–1 in the final.

Diego Maradona, *second from right*, competes against members of England's team during a 1986 World Cup quarterfinal. Maradona scored two memorable goals during the match.

1980s–EARLY 1990s

The World Cup returned to Europe in 1982, with Spain serving as the host. The West German team arrived as defending European champions. It slipped past France in a shoot-out in one semifinal. In the other, Italy defeated Poland. In the final, the Italians made three second-half goals to clinch their third World Cup.

Colombia was supposed to host the 1986 World Cup. But economic crises forced FIFA to move the Cup to Mexico. The tournament was a showcase for Argentina's striker Diego Maradona. He scored five goals, including two in the quarterfinals against England. In the final, Maradona set up Jorge Burruchaga for the game-winning goal in the eighty-fourth minute. Argentina won its second World Cup, beating West Germany.

During the 1990 World Cup, hosted in Italy, Cameroon became the first African team to reach the quarterfinals. Both semifinals went to shoot-outs after 120 minutes. Argentina defeated Italy, while West Germany beat England. In the final, West Germany faced off against Argentina. West Germany won, with the match's only goal coming on a penalty kick in the eighty-fifth minute.

AWARDS

After each World Cup, awards are presented to teams and players. The tournament's best player receives the Golden Ball, an award established in 1982. Runners-up receive the Silver Ball and Bronze Ball. Whoever scores the most goals in the Cup wins the Golden Boot. In 2022, Kylian Mbappé won the Golden Boot. Other tournaments give out similar awards.

Cameroon's François Omam-Biyik, *right*, celebrates after scoring a goal during a 1990 World Cup match against Argentina. Cameroon won the match 1–0.

MID- TO LATE 1990s

In 1994, the United States hosted the World Cup for the first time. Its team also advanced to the knockout rounds for the first time. But the Americans lost 1–0 to Brazil. It was the first of three straight one-goal wins that put Brazil in the final. It faced off against Italy, which had also won several close matches. The final remained scoreless after 120 minutes. In the first penalty shoot-out in World Cup final history, Brazil won 3–2. The tournament gave American audiences their first taste of international soccer. This led to the creation of MLS and a major foothold for the sport in the United States.

Brazilian goalie Cláudio Taffarel, *center left*, dives to block the ball as Italy's Roberto Baggio, *center right*, attempts to score. Baggio ended up missing the goal.

French team captain Didier Deschamps, *holding trophy*, celebrates with his teammates after winning the 1998 World Cup final.

In 1998, the tournament was held in France. The number of teams expanded to 32, increasing from six to eight groups. The host team was dominant in group play, but it needed extra time to defeat Paraguay in the first knockout round. France defeated Italy in the quarterfinals and beat Croatia in the semifinals. In the final, France defeated Brazil 3–0 to win its first World Cup title.

Brazil's Ronaldo, *left*, competes against members of the German team during the 2002 World Cup. Ronaldo scored both goals in Brazil's 2–0 victory.

EARLY 2000s

The 2002 World Cup in Japan and South Korea was historic. It was the first World Cup in Asia. It was also the first hosted by two countries. Defending champion France got shut out in all three group matches. South Korea was the biggest surprise of the tournament. It defeated Italy and Spain before losing to Germany in the semifinals. In the final, Brazil beat Germany 2–0.

In the 2006 Cup in Germany, European teams reigned supreme again. Italy faced off against France in the final. The match was marred when Frenchman Zinedine Zidane received a red card after headbutting an opponent. After playing to a 1–1 draw through 120 minutes, Italy won 5–3. It was the country's first World Cup title in 24 years.

In 2010, the World Cup took place in Africa for the first time. The event was known for the vuvuzela, a plastic horn popular with South African fans. The instrument created a droning buzz in stadiums that was sometimes deafening. Spain won, with Andrés Iniesta's goal in extra time giving his team a 1–0 victory over the Netherlands.

Andrés Iniesta, *right*, takes his game-winning shot during the 2010 World Cup final. The goal happened in extra time in the 116th minute of the match.

THE 2010s–2020s

During the 2014 World Cup, host team Brazil had high hopes. But these hopes were dashed when the team's striker Neymar was injured in the quarterfinals. In the next round, Brazil suffered a 7–1 defeat by Germany. In the final, Germany faced off against Argentina. Mario Götze scored the only goal in extra time. That made Germany the first European team to win the World Cup on South American soil.

For the 2018 World Cup in Russia, video assistant referee (VAR) was used during the tournament for the first time. This technology helps referees review video footage of gameplay. It figured into many results, granting officials second looks at

Kylian Mbappé kisses the trophy after leading France to victory in the 2018 World Cup final. The match took place at Luzhniki Stadium in Moscow, Russia.

Argentina's national team celebrates after winning a 2022 World Cup semifinal. The team defeated Croatia 3–0 to earn a spot in the final.

controversial calls. Croatia reached the final for the first time. But France, led by Kylian Mbappé, coasted to a 4–2 victory in the final.

The year 2022 marked the first time the World Cup was played in winter. Temperatures in host country Qatar were too hot for the usual schedule. The choice of host was controversial, too. Qatar had been criticized for human rights violations of migrant workers who were building stadiums for the tournament. France and Argentina met in a memorable final. Argentina won, giving Lionel Messi his first major international trophy.

Members of the US team pose for a photo during the 1991 Women's World Cup in Guangdong, China. April Heinrichs, *back row left*, served as team captain.

WOMEN'S WORLD CUP

By the 1970s, women had gained more opportunities to play sports. That momentum continued throughout the 1980s. FIFA organized the first Women's World Cup in 1991. China, the host team, was one of 12 participants. China, the United States, and Germany won their groups, setting up a memorable knockout phase. Sweden defeated China 1–0 in the only quarterfinal upset. But Sweden was then defeated by its rival, Norway. In the other semifinal, the United States routed Germany 5–2. In the final, US captain Michelle Akers scored twice. With a 2–1 victory, the USWNT became the first Women's World Cup champions.

The 1995 Women's World Cup was a prelude to the first appearance of women's soccer at the Olympics in 1996.

The tournament was held in Sweden. The defending champions defeated Japan 4–0 in the quarterfinals. But Norway got revenge in the semifinals, defeating the United States. In the final, Norway scored two goals late in the first half, securing a 2–0 victory over Germany.

Teams must qualify for the Women's World Cup. In 2023, the tournament followed a similar structure to past men's World Cups. It featured 32 teams divided into eight groups of four. Teams played against others in their group, and the top two from each group advanced to the knockout stage. Teams moved through knockout stages until reaching a final two.

Norway's Linda Medalen, *left*, races after Sweden's Anette Hansson, *right*, during a 1991 Women's World Cup semifinal match.

1999 WOMEN'S WORLD CUP

The 1996 Olympics in Atlanta, Georgia, put women's soccer on the world stage. The US team created buzz with its gold-medal performance. Three summers later, in 1999, the Women's World Cup was held on US soil for the first time. The US team hoped to avenge its 1995 defeat and show that its Olympic success was not a fluke. The team carried the hopes of millions of American soccer fans.

For the first time, all 32 tournament games were shown live on TV. Huge audiences tuned in on TV, while crowds filled stadiums throughout the country. The United States advanced

A record 90,185 people attended the 1999 Women's World Cup final at the Rose Bowl in Pasadena, California. The attendance number appeared on a scoreboard during the match.

US goalie Briana Scurry blocks China's penalty shoot-out attempt during the 1999 Women's World Cup final. Scurry's save helped the USWNT win the match.

through the knockout stage with tight wins over Germany and Brazil.

In the final, the US team faced off against China. The match was held at the Rose Bowl in Pasadena, California. More than 90,000 fans attended. The rivals battled to a scoreless draw, sending the final to a shoot-out.

After each team scored on their first two kicks, US goalie Briana Scurry made a diving stop on a kick from China's Liu Ying. The next four shooters scored, meaning the result depended on Brandi Chastain's final attempt. She calmly buried it. Her teammates charged to celebrate as the United States became the first to win two Women's World Cups.

EARLY 2000s

German Birgit Prinz was awarded the Golden Ball after her team won the Women's World Cup in 2003. Prinz also won the Golden Boot that year.

The 2003 Women's World Cup was originally scheduled to take place in China. However, an outbreak of the disease SARS in China forced FIFA to move the Cup to the United States. After coasting through group play, the US team's dream of defending its title was crushed in a 3–0 loss to Germany. In the final, Germany's Nia Künzer scored a goal in the ninety-eighth minute, giving her team a 2–1 victory over Sweden. The tournament marked a passing of the torch for the USWNT, as many stars from its 1990s teams soon retired from international play.

In 2007, China hosted the tournament again. Germany was determined to become the first team to win two Women's World Cups in a row. The Germans began in style, securing an 11–0 victory over Argentina in the opening match. Their biggest threat was Brazil, whose budding star Marta earned the

Golden Ball as the tournament's best player. She made two of her seven goals in a semifinal against the United States. Brazil won the match 4–0. But Germany defeated Brazil in the final.

Germany's national team celebrates after winning the 2007 Women's World Cup. The final match took place in Shanghai, China.

THE 2010s

The 2011 Women's World Cup, hosted by Germany, is best remembered for a goal in the quarterfinals. Abby Wambach's header off a long Megan Rapinoe cross pulled the US team even with Brazil in the 121st minute. The Americans won in a shoot-out. But they were on the other end of a shocking sequence in the final against Japan.

Homare Sawa was a key player in Japan's 2011 Women's World Cup victory. That year, she received multiple awards and was named the FIFA Women's World Player of the Year.

Abby Wambach falls to her knees after winning the 2015 World Cup final at BC Place Stadium in Vancouver, Canada.

Another Wambach goal in extra time appeared to give the Americans the victory. But Japan's Homare Sawa tied the game. Japan ended up winning in a shoot-out, becoming the first Asian country to win a World Cup.

Canada hosted the 2015 tournament, during which the US team quickly proved itself to be a world power. The Americans defeated the three previous champions. The US team and its goalie Hope Solo shut out Germany 2–0 in the semifinals. In the final, the US team stunned Japan with four goals in the first 16 minutes. US captain Carli Lloyd scored three of them, including one launched from near midfield. The 5–2 victory made the Americans the first three-time Women's World Cup champions.

The official slogan of the 2019 Women's World Cup was "Dare to Shine." The slogan appeared throughout the Stade de Lyon stadium as the US team celebrated its fourth World Cup victory.

THE 2020s

In 2019, the Women's World Cup was held in France. The USWNT had never won consecutive World Cups. That year, the team tried to change that with a dominant run through group play. In the knockout rounds, the US team posted three straight 2–1 victories over Spain, France, and England. That put the Americans in the final against the Netherlands, a team making its first appearance on the big stage. US forward Megan Rapinoe converted a penalty kick in the sixty-first minute.

Eight minutes later, Rose Lavelle added a goal, and the United States secured a 2–0 victory.

The year 2023 marked the first World Cup in Oceania. Australia and New Zealand were hosts. The tournament brought new faces into the spotlight. The two-time defending champions were eliminated by Sweden on penalties in the Round of 16. This round happens between the group stage and quarterfinals, when 16 teams remain.

Until its 2023 victory, Spain had never made it to the quarterfinals of the Women's World Cup.

Australia made it further into the tournament than ever before. But Australia lost to England in the semifinals. Spain defeated Sweden in the other semifinal, creating the first matchup of two first-time finalists since the inaugural 1991 Cup. Olga Carmona scored the only goal in Spain's 1–0 victory.

MEN'S CONTINENTAL CHAMPIONSHIPS

The men's World Cup happens once every four years. But in between those years, fans have other opportunities to cheer on national teams. Each continental confederation sanctions competitions between national teams in that continent or region. These tournaments allow fans to follow their favorite players and teams. They also give teams from smaller countries chances to shine. Iceland, for example, had a surprise run to the quarterfinals at the 2016 European Championship.

FIFA oversees six continental confederations, each of which runs its own championship tournament. One is the European

Iceland's Ragnar Sigurðsson, *left*, and Aron Gunnarsson, *center*, face off against Portugal's Cristiano Ronaldo, *right*, during a Euro group stage match in 2016. The match ended with a score of 1–1.

Italy, *blue*, and England, *white*, face off in the 2020 Euro final. Italy defeated England in a penalty shoot-out.

Championship, or the Euro. It began in 1960, with the Soviet Union winning the first title. The tournament has since expanded to 24 teams, with 55 member nations attempting to qualify. The Euro takes place every four years. Spain won its third European title in 2012, tying Germany for the most wins ever.

NATIONS LEAGUE

The Nations League is a biennial men's soccer tournament featuring UEFA members. It was first held in 2018 to fill time between the Euros and World Cup. The organization's 55 member teams are split into four leagues based on rank. Within these leagues, teams are put into groups. Winners of group matches move to knockout stages. In 2023, Spain won the Nations League.

Lionel Messi, *center*, poses with the trophy after Argentina's victory in the 2021 Copa América final. The team defeated Brazil 1–0 in the match.

Copa América is the championship of South American soccer. Its confederation is Confederación Sudamericana de Fútbol, or CONMEBOL. CONMEBOL includes ten teams, so outside countries are invited to fill out the Copa América field. The competition dates back to 1916. In 2011, Uruguay won its fifteenth Copa América. Argentina tied that number in 2021.

CONCACAF includes North America, Central America, and Caribbean countries. Its championship is the Gold Cup. It's played every two years. In 2023, Mexico won its ninth Gold Cup. The United States won its seventh in 2021.

The Asian Football Confederation (AFC) hosts the Asian Cup. It began in 1956, with South Korea winning. The event happens every four years. In 2011, Japan won its fourth Asian Cup. As of 2023, this is the most any participant has won.

The Confederation of African Football (CAF) holds the Africa Cup of Nations every two years. Egypt won the first Africa Cup title in 1957. In 2010, the country won a seventh time, the most championships of any participant.

The Oceania Football Confederation (OFC) features New Zealand and South Pacific island nations. Australia was a founding member in 1966 but joined AFC in 2006. The OFC Men's Nations Cup was first held in 1973. New Zealand won its fifth Men's Nations Cup title in 2016.

The Ivory Coast's Franck Kessie, *left*, squares off against Nigeria's Ademola Lookman, *right*, during the final match of the 2023 Africa Cup of Nations. The Ivory Coast won 2–1.

WOMEN'S CONTINENTAL CHAMPIONSHIPS

In women's soccer, continental championships are a more recent development. But three of them predate the first Women's World Cup. The first women's continental championship was the Women's Asian Cup. It began in 1975 and has been played at different intervals ever since. Since 2010, it has taken place every four years. In 2022, China won its ninth Women's Asian Cup. In 2023, officials changed the schedule so the tournament would happen in odd-numbered years between Women's World Cups. That meant the next Asian Cups would be in 2026 and 2029.

The OFC Women's Nations Cup debuted in 1983. The Women's Nations Cup has since been held every three or four years, except between 1998 and 2003. The 2022 tournament

Members of China's team race across the field after defeating Japan in a 2022 Women's Asian Cup semifinal. China went on to defeat South Korea in the final.

England's Chloe Kelly, *right*, squares off against Germany's Kathrin Hendrich, *left*, during the final match of the 2022 Women's Euro. Kelly went on to score the game-winning goal for England.

was held in Fiji, with Papua New Guinea winning its first championship. New Zealand holds the most titles with six.

Next came the European Women's Championship, or Women's Euro, in 1984. It is one of the biggest events on the women's soccer calendar. Sweden defeated England to win the first championship. Between 1987 and 2001, the event was held every two years. It switched to a four-year cycle in 2001. Germany has won the most championships with eight. In 2022, host country England won the final in front of more than 87,000 fans at Wembley Stadium. This was a record for a men's or women's Euro match.

In 2022, the CONCACAF W Championship final was held at BBVA Stadium in Monterrey, Mexico. The United States defeated Canada 1–0.

Three more women's continental championships debuted in 1991, the same year as the first Women's World Cup. CONCACAF's women's tournament has had several different names, but it was called the CONCACAF W Championship in 2022. The United States has dominated the competition, winning nine of 11 titles through 2022. Canada won the other two titles.

CAF sponsors the Women's Africa Cup of Nations. Since 1998, the competition has been held every two years. Nigeria won 11 of the first 13 championships, with Equatorial Guinea

taking the other two. In 2022, South Africa took home its first title, defeating Morocco 2–1 in the final.

CONMEBOL teams play for the Copa América Femenina, or Women's Copa América. It first took place in 1991. Since 2006, it's been played every four years. Brazil has won eight of the nine titles through 2022. Argentina is the only other country to win. It hosted the tournament in 2006, defeating Brazil in the final.

Brazil's team celebrates after winning the 2022 Copa América Femenina. The team defeated Colombia to claim the title.

SOCCER PYRAMIDS

Most countries have multiple levels of soccer league competition. This is often called a pyramid or ladder. For example, England has the men's Premier League, which includes the country's top 20 clubs. Below the Premier League is the Championship, which includes the next best 24 clubs. League 1 and League 2 are the third and fourth tiers. Below that, the National League is the top level of a system of professional and semipro leagues organized by region. Teams at the bottom of the National League, including

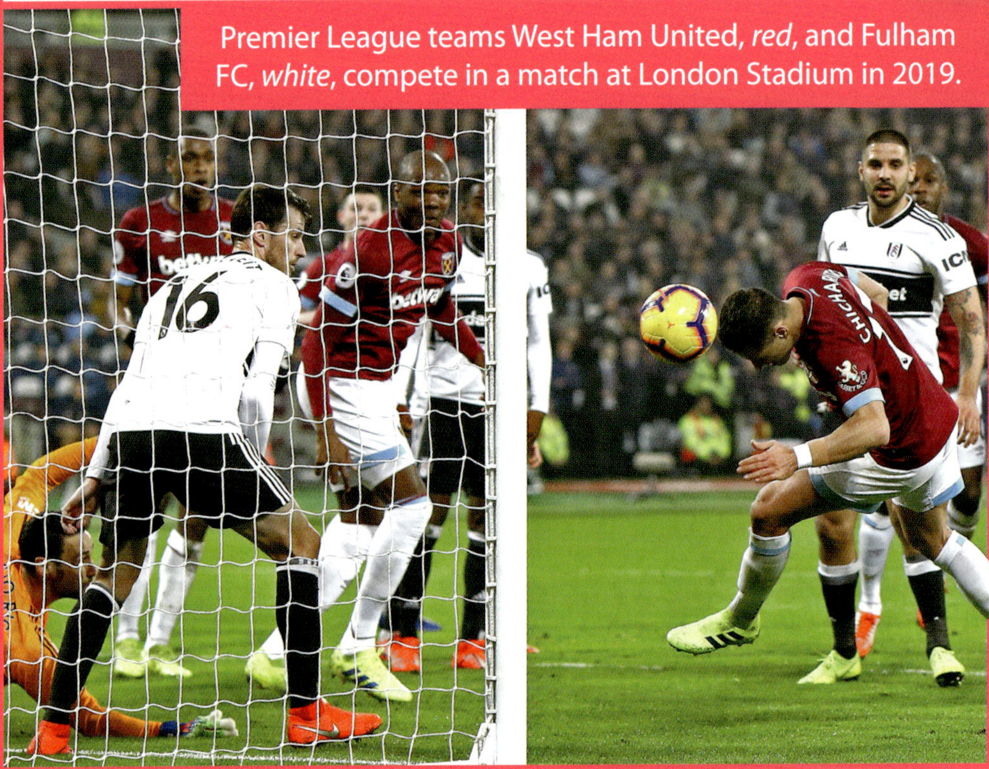

Premier League teams West Ham United, *red*, and Fulham FC, *white*, compete in a match at London Stadium in 2019.

Minnesota United FC's Tani Oluwaseyi, *right*, squares off against Atlanta United FC's Noah Cobb, *left*, during a 2024 match in Atlanta, Georgia. Minnesota defeated Atlanta 2–1.

National League North and National League South, fall into the sixth and seventh tiers.

During the regular season, clubs compete with the goal of finishing at or near the top of their league standings. The best clubs are promoted, meaning they get to move up a step on the ladder. Clubs that perform poorly are relegated, or bumped down a level.

Other countries have similar pyramids. In the United States, the top tier is MLS. Below that is the USL Championship, followed by USL League 1, National Independent Soccer Association (NISA), and MLS Next Pro. The next tier includes amateur leagues, while the bottom tier includes college soccer associations.

Members of DC United pose with the Alan I. Rothenberg Trophy after winning the first MLS Cup in 1996. The final match took place in Foxborough, Massachusetts.

MAJOR LEAGUE SOCCER

In 1988, FIFA awarded the United States the rights to host the 1994 men's World Cup. One of its requirements, however, was that the United States commit to creating a top-tier pro men's soccer league. The North American Soccer League (NASL) had thrived at times during the 1970s. However, the country had been without a top-level league since the NASL folded in 1985.

MLS FOUNDING TEAMS

- **Tampa Bay Mutiny**
- **Dallas Burn** (later renamed FC Dallas)
- **Colorado Rapids**
- **New England Revolution**
- **DC United**
- **Columbus Crew**
- **Kansas City Wiz** (later renamed Sporting Kansas City)
- **NY/NJ MetroStars** (later renamed the New York Red Bulls)
- **Los Angeles Galaxy**
- **San Jose Clash** (later renamed San Jose Earthquakes)

The result was MLS. It debuted in 1996 with ten teams. American audiences weren't accustomed to some of soccer's rules. So MLS made a few tweaks to make fans more comfortable and generate interest in the sport.

For instance, unlike most American sports, soccer uses a clock that counts up from 0:00. MLS reversed that, with the clock counting down from 45:00 each half. Penalty shoot-outs were used to break all ties. And instead of using the traditional spot kick from 12 yards (11 m) out, MLS shoot-outs started with the ball 35 yards (32 m) from the goal. The attacker had five seconds to dribble in and take a shot. These early rules are no longer in place.

As of 2023, California team LA Galaxy has won the most MLS Cups with five. Their latest victory came in 2014.

Like other new pro sports leagues, MLS lost money in its first few years. But most teams survived, and the league began to grow in its second decade. Compared to the biggest leagues in Europe and South America, MLS was still considered a minor league. But that began to change in 2007. That's when English superstar David Beckham signed a five-year contract with LA Galaxy. Suddenly, one of Europe's biggest stars was playing in the United States. Even though he was in the latter stages of his career, Beckham's presence helped MLS gain global recognition.

David Beckham left Real Madrid to play for LA Galaxy. He played with the team from 2007 to 2012.

Lionel Messi, *front row left*, poses with his Inter Miami teammates before a 2024 match in Canada. He wears a number 10 shirt on the team, the same number he wore while playing for previous teams.

Other world stars soon followed in Beckham's footsteps. Thierry Henry from France, David Villa from Spain, Bastian Schweinsteiger from Germany, Kaká from Brazil, Wayne Rooney from England, and Zlatan Ibrahimović from Sweden were among the greats who thrilled fans in MLS games. Meanwhile, several top US stars shone in MLS, including Landon Donovan, Clint Dempsey, Eddie Pope, and Brian McBride. When Argentine legend Lionel Messi joined Inter Miami in 2023, the soccer world took notice again. MLS continued to grow.

MLS FAST FACTS

First season: 1996

First champion: DC United

Most titles: 5, LA Galaxy

Most goals, season: 34, Carlos Vela, LAFC (2019)

Most goals, career: 174, Chris Wondolowski

* Statistics through 2023

Members of the Los Angeles Sol race across the field during the first WPS match in 2009. The team faced off against the Washington Freedom.

NATIONAL WOMEN'S SOCCER LEAGUE

Interest in women's soccer took off in the United States after the country hosted the 1999 Women's World Cup. Creating women's professional leagues proved challenging, however. The Women's United Soccer Association (WUSA) started play in 2001, filling its rosters with stars from the USWNT. But after struggling financially, the WUSA shut down after three seasons.

In 2009, Women's Professional Soccer (WPS) began play. Again, top players from the USWNT and other countries participated. But like the WUSA, WPS shut down after three seasons due to legal and financial problems.

A new league was launched immediately. This time, it had better financial backing. The National Women's Soccer League (NWSL) had financial support from the national soccer federations in the United States, Canada, and Mexico. As a result, it began play on firmer ground than the WUSA or WPS had.

Abby Wambach competes for the Western New York Flash during a 2013 NWSL match in Rochester, New York.

Under a unique partnership, the national federations paid NWSL the salaries of any players from their national team rosters. This made it easier for teams to field competitive lineups. The big-name players and increased level of competition generated more excitement and publicity for the league.

The first NWSL champions were a perfect example. Portland Thorns FC's two leading scorers were Canada's Christine Sinclair and the USWNT's Alex Morgan. Both were already stars for their national teams. In the league final, the two players worked together on the last goal to secure a 2–0 victory over the Western New York Flash. This team featured US stars Abby Wambach and Carli Lloyd as well as Australian Sam Kerr.

Portland Thorns members Alex Morgan, *left*, and Christine Sinclair, *right*, smile after winning the first NWSL Championship in 2013. They defeated the Western New York Flash 2–0 to claim the title.

San Diego Wave FC's Naomi Girma competes during an NWSL match in 2024. The team went on to defeat Gotham FC 1–0.

The Portland Thorns proved to be the NWSL's early power, winning three of the first ten league championships. But the league has continued to improve. In 2022, Angel City FC (Los Angeles) and San Diego Wave FC joined the league. With backing from celebrities and other pro athletes, these teams drew huge crowds. Their success helped show that the NWSL was a popular and growing league.

NWSL FAST FACTS

First season: 2013

First champion: Portland Thorns FC

Most titles: 3, Portland Thorns FC

Most goals, season: 18, Sam Kerr, Chicago Red Stars (2019)

Most goals, career: 79, Lynn Williams

* Statistics through 2024

LIGA MX

Members of Pumas UNAM celebrate after defeating Necaxa in a 2021 Liga MX match. Pumas UNAM won the match 1–0.

Formerly known as the Primera División, Liga MX is the top men's soccer league in Mexico. Its schedule is divided into two seasons. The *apertura*, or "opening," runs from July to December. The *clausura*, or "closing," is played between January and May. The champion of each season is determined by a playoff tournament called a *liguilla*.

Liga MX dates back to the 1940s. But Europeans had introduced soccer to locals in Mexico near the turn of the century. Four decades of amateur soccer led to the creation of the first professional league in 1943. The sport's popularity in Mexico soared after the country hosted the 1970 World Cup.

LIGA MX FAST FACTS

First season: 1943–44

First champion: Asturias

Most titles: 15, Club América

Most goals, season: 40, Roberto Aballay, Asturias (1944–45), Isidro Lángara, RC España (1945–46)

Most goals, career: 312, Evanivaldo Castro Silva (Cabinho)

* Statistics through 2024

Since then, Liga MX has grown into the third-most-attended sports league in North America, trailing only the National Football League (NFL) and Major League Baseball (MLB). Top teams in Liga MX include Club América, Guadalajara, and CF Pachuca. América and Guadalajara have a famous rivalry.

In 2024, Club América took home the Liga MX Clausura title. The team defeated Cruz Azul to claim the title.

PREMIER LEAGUE

Compared with other European leagues, the English Premier League is relatively new. For a long time, England's top men's league was called the First Division. However, public interest in soccer dwindled during the 1980s. Attendance was lagging. Rowdy fans gave English soccer a bad name with destructive behavior at home and at games abroad. The First Division even began the 1985–86 season without a TV deal.

The EFL managed the First Division. But top club owners were not happy with EFL leaders. In February 1992, all 22 First Division clubs resigned from EFL. Three months later, the Premier League was born.

Everton FC was one of the 22 original members of the Premier League. As of 2024, the team has been based at Goodison Park, a stadium in Liverpool, England.

In 1993, Manchester United became the first team to win the Premier League. Team members Steve Bruce, *left*, and Bryan Robson, *right*, posed with the trophy after winning the title.

In some ways, the Premier League looked much like the First Division. Both sat atop England's soccer pyramid. Each season, teams at the bottom of the standings were relegated to the second division. But the Premier League had more control over its operations. It pursued a more aggressive TV strategy. Thanks to advancements in cable and satellite TV, fans worldwide could easily watch Premier League matches. This generated more money, which teams used to sign better players. The Premier League quickly became the world's richest league.

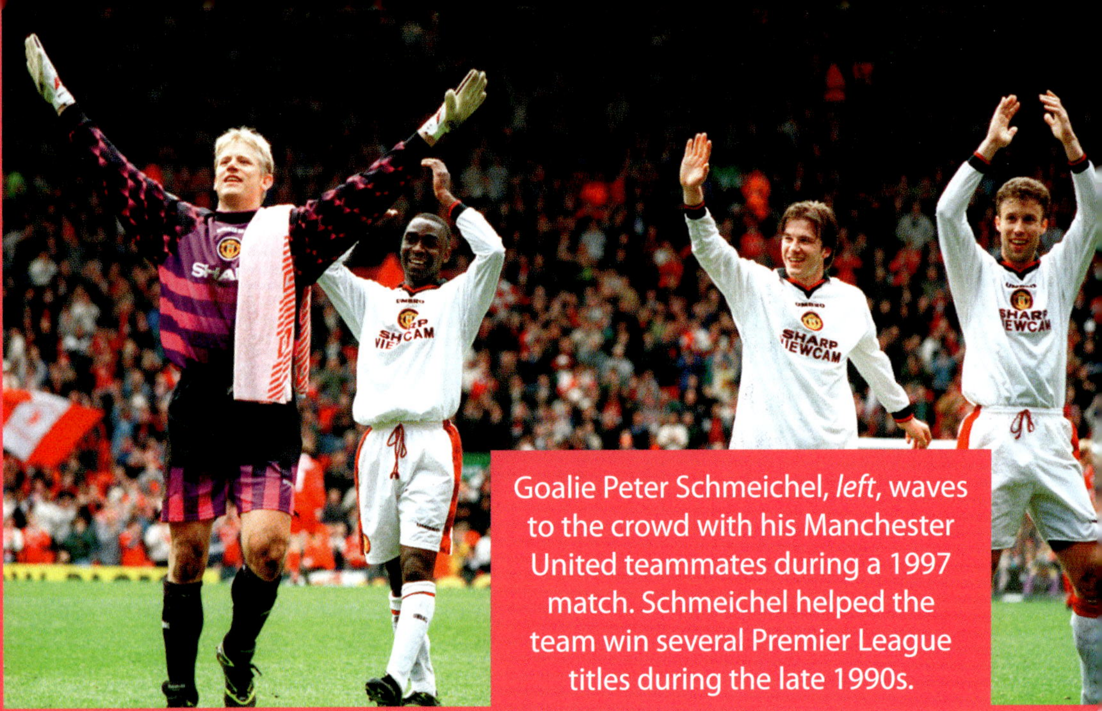

Goalie Peter Schmeichel, *left*, waves to the crowd with his Manchester United teammates during a 1997 match. Schmeichel helped the team win several Premier League titles during the late 1990s.

Manchester United had been one of England's top teams prior to the Premier League's founding. Under legendary manager Sir Alex Ferguson, United became the first superpower in the Premier League. The Red Devils won seven of the first nine Premier League titles. Their star players included David Beckham, Gary Neville, Roy Keane, Andy Cole, and goalie Peter Schmeichel.

In 2003–04, Arsenal went through an entire season without a loss. The Gunners won 26 matches, while the other 12 ended in draws. The team, known as "The Invincibles,"

PREMIER LEAGUE FAST FACTS

First season: 1992–93

First champion: Manchester United

Most titles: 13, Manchester United

Most goals, season: 36, Erling Haaland, Manchester City (2022–23)

Most goals, career: 260, Alan Shearer

* Statistics through 2024

remained the Premier League's only undefeated team two decades later. However, Manchester United and Chelsea soon emerged as the dominant teams for the rest of the decade.

In the 2010s, Manchester City became the team to beat, thanks in part to its commitment to bringing in the best international talent. In the 2017–18 season, the Cityzens, whose roster included players from 11 countries, became the first Premier League team to post a 100-point season. It had 32 wins, four draws, and two losses. It was the team's first of six titles over the next seven seasons.

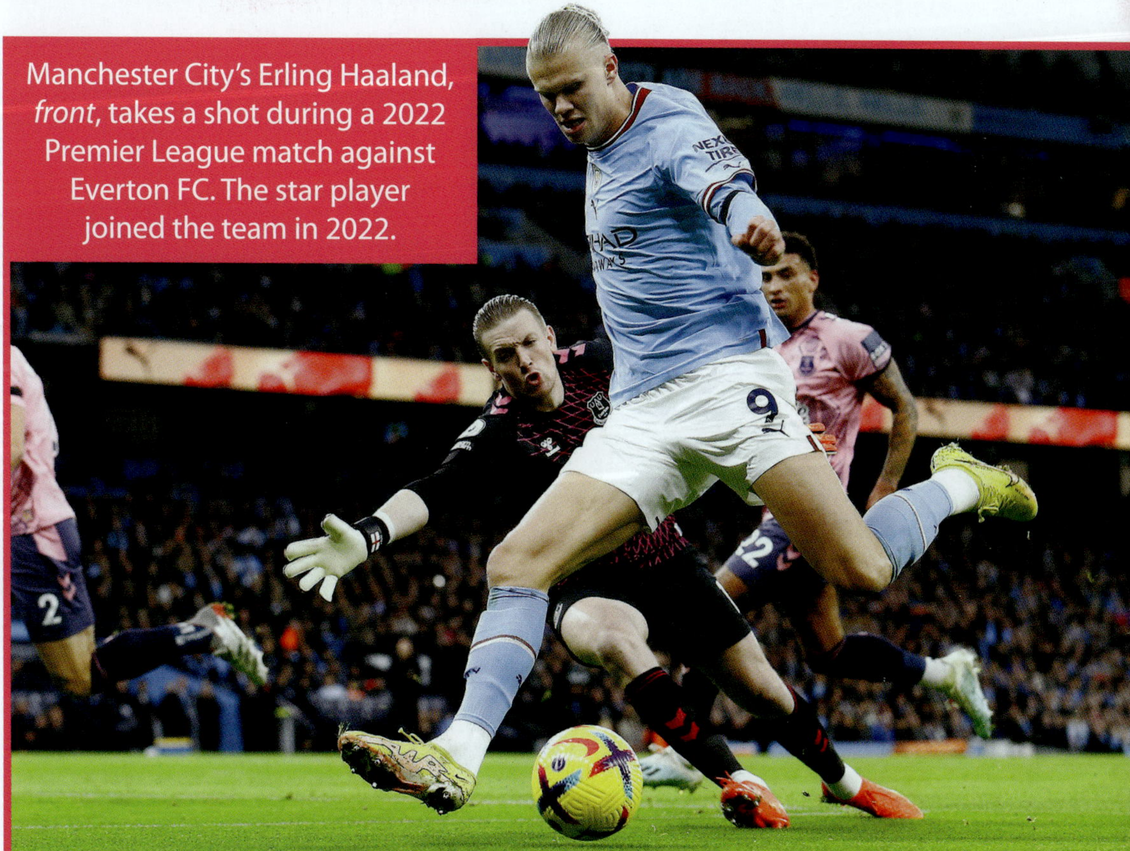

Manchester City's Erling Haaland, *front*, takes a shot during a 2022 Premier League match against Everton FC. The star player joined the team in 2022.

LA LIGA

Few leagues have boasted as much star power as La Liga, the top league in Spain. It was founded in 1929 and has been mostly dominated by two clubs: Real Madrid and FC Barcelona. Through La Liga's first 95 years, only nine clubs had won the league championship. Madrid and Barcelona won a combined total of 63 titles. Atlético Madrid was next with ten championships, followed by Athletic Bilbao with eight and Valencia with six. No other club had more than two titles.

Real Madrid's Alfredo Di Stéfano competed in many La Liga matches. Di Stéfano played with Real Madrid for 11 years.

Iker Casillas, *center*, holds up the La Liga trophy after Real Madrid claimed the title in 2012. It was the team's thirty-second La Liga victory.

Real Madrid began its climb to becoming the world's top club in the 1950s. Two of the game's biggest stars, Argentine Alfredo Di Stéfano and Hungarian Ferenc Puskás, helped Real Madrid win four La Liga titles during the decade. But Madrid's biggest feats were accomplished elsewhere on the continent. The European Cup, now known as the UEFA Champions League, began in 1955–56. Real Madrid won the first five competitions. The team won its thirteenth European title in 2022, giving it twice as many wins as the next-best team.

Real Madrid's Karim Benzema, *right*, competes during a 2014 La Liga match against Barcelona. The striker helped Real Madrid claim four La Liga titles.

Real Madrid is famous for bringing in superstar players. In the 2000s, the team's *Galácticos* included Ronaldo, David Beckham, and Zinedine Zidane. Superstars such as Cristiano Ronaldo, Karim Benzema, and Vinicius Junior took over in the 2010s. Barcelona has been no stranger to foreign talent, either. Johan Cruyff, Luis Suárez, Ronaldinho, and Neymar are just a few great players who have worn Barcelona's blue-and-garnet uniforms.

For years, the *El Clásico* rivalry between Barcelona and Madrid has dominated La Liga. During the 2010s, that rivalry grew to include expected showdowns between two of the world's best players. Barcelona's Lionel Messi and Madrid's

Cristiano Ronaldo battled for supremacy. Because of this, every match between the clubs seemed important.

Politics also lend an edge to the rivalry. Real Madrid plays in Spain's capital city and is associated with the Spanish royalty and government. Barcelona is the country's second-largest city and is located in the Catalonia region. For nearly two centuries, people in Catalonia have pushed to become independent from Spain. The club has become a symbol of that effort.

LA LIGA FAST FACTS

First season: 1929–30

First champion: Barcelona

Most titles: 36, Real Madrid

Most goals, season: 50, Lionel Messi, Barcelona (2011–12)

Most goals, career: 474, Lionel Messi

* Statistics through 2024

The *El Clásico* rivalry between Barcelona and Real Madrid dates back to the early 1900s and has continued into the 2020s. *El Clásico* is Spanish for "The Classic."

SERIE A (ITALY)

Italy has a rich soccer history. Many passionate fans support the Italian men's national team, one of the most successful in the world. Most players who have won trophies for Italy also play in Serie A, the country's top men's soccer league.

THE SCUDETTO

The team that wins Serie A earns the *scudetto*, which means "little shield" in Italian. The *scudetto* is a badge featuring the colors of the Italian flag, which are red, green, and white. Serie A champions proudly wear the badge on their jerseys during the next season.

Members of Inter Milan celebrate their victory over AC Milan in the 2024 Serie A. The match took place at San Siro Stadium in Milan, Italy.

Juventus captain Giorgio Chiellini, *holding trophy*, celebrates with his teammates after winning the 2019 Serie A. The Serie A trophy is known as the Coppa Campioni d'Italia.

The most successful club in Serie A history has been Juventus, which is based in Turin. This city is the cultural and economic center of northern Italy. Over the years, a natural rivalry developed between two clubs that play in Milan, which is located 87 miles (140 km) to the east. In 2024, Inter Milan won the Serie A title for the twentieth time, breaking its tie with AC Milan's 19 wins. Juventus, with 36 titles, has won almost as many titles as the two Milan teams combined.

Parma's star goalie Gianluigi Buffon competes during a Serie A match against AC Milan in 1998. Buffon was only 17 when he made his Serie A debut with the team.

Many of Italy's greatest players have starred for Serie A clubs. Legendary goalkeeper Gianluigi Buffon debuted in 1998 with Parma. He retired 25 years later, having spent 19 seasons playing for Juventus. Only forward Alessandro Del Piero, who was with the team from 1993 to 2012, played in more games for Juventus. Defender Paolo Maldini spent his entire 21-year career with AC Milan. He retired in 2009. Francesco Totti played for Roma from 1992 to 2017.

Juventus won a record nine straight Serie A titles from 2012 to 2020. But the club has been no stranger to scandal. In 2006, Juventus was stripped of points and relegated to the second division, Serie B, after being caught in a shocking plot to influence the outcome of matches. This opened the door for Inter Milan to win five straight titles as Juventus struggled to regain its footing.

SERIE A FAST FACTS

First season: 1929–30

First champion: Inter Milan

Most titles: 36, Juventus*

Most goals, season: 36, Gino Rossetti, Torino (1928–29); Gonzalo Higuaín, Napoli (2015–16); Ciro Immobile, Lazio (2019–20)

Most goals, career: 274, Silvio Piola

* Serie A recognizes all first-tier champions before the league was founded. Statistics through 2024

Juventus's Federico Chiesa celebrates after scoring a goal during a 2024 Serie A match. After just one season in Serie B, the team returned to its Serie A status for the 2007–08 season.

LIGUE 1

France's top men's division has been known as Ligue 1 since 2002. But the country has a rich history of supporting high-level soccer. The contributions of French players have also been vital to the league. Midfielder Didier Deschamps, striker Thierry Henry, and striker Kylian Mbappé are just a few of the greats who have won Ligue 1 titles and the World Cup for France.

In 2024, Paris Saint-Germain (PSG) won a record twelfth Ligue 1 title. But PSG's dominance has been a recent development. Beginning in

Paris Saint-Germain's Kylian Mbappé takes a shot during a Ligue 1 match against Clermont in 2024. Mbappé has helped the team claim several Ligue 1 titles.

In 2024, Paris Saint-Germain celebrated its Ligue 1 victory at the Parc de Princes stadium in Paris, France.

the 2012–13 season, the team won ten of the next 12 championships. Before that stretch, many clubs had periods of major success. Lyon won the league for seven straight years beginning in the 2001–02 season. Saint-Étienne won four straight titles in the 1960s. From 1989 to 1992, Marseille matched that run.

LIGUE 1 FAST FACTS

First season: 1932–33

First champion: Olympique Lillois

Most titles: 12, Paris Saint-Germain

Most goals, season: 44, Josip Skoblar, Marseille (1970–71)

Most goals, career: 299, Delio Onnis

* Statistics through 2024

Borussia Dortmund's Christian Pulisic, *left*, squares off against Eintracht Frankfurt's Timothy Chandler, *right*, during a 2016 Bundesliga match. Both Dortmund and Frankfurt are top teams in the Bundesliga.

BUNDESLIGA

Germany has made substantial contributions to the soccer world. Some of the greatest men's soccer stars have played in the country's top division, the Bundesliga. Defender Franz Beckenbauer, striker Gerd Müller, and goalkeeper Manuel Neuer are some of the legendary players who have starred for both club and country.

Not surprisingly, all three players starred for Bayern Munich. One of the world's top clubs, Bayern has dominated the Bundesliga. In its most recent era of success, the club started a run of 11 straight titles in the 2012–13 season. During that span, Bayern won a treble—or three trophies in one season—two times. The three trophies were the league title, Germany's domestic cup, and the UEFA Champions League. Other top German clubs include Borussia Dortmund, Werder Bremen, VfB Stuttgart, and Bayer Leverkusen.

BUNDESLIGA FAST FACTS

First season: 1963–64

First champion: FC Cologne

Most titles: 32, Bayern Munich

Most goals, season: 41, Robert Lewandowski, Bayern Munich (2020–21)

Most goals, career: 365, Gerd Müller

* Statistics through 2024

Jamal Musiala, *center*, celebrates after scoring the game-winning goal for Bayern Munich during a 2023 Bundesliga match. The team won its eleventh title that year.

EREDIVISIE

The top men's soccer league in the Netherlands is the Eredivisie. It has been the proving ground for generations of talented Dutch players. It's impossible to discuss the history of soccer in the Netherlands without focusing on Johan Cruyff. The three-time European Footballer of the Year starred for Ajax in the 1960s and early 1970s. His ideas and playing style influenced the sport far beyond the country's borders.

Striker Marco van Basten, defender Ruud Gullit, and midfielder Frank Rijkaard were other Dutch greats. They all

Ajax's Johan Cruyff, *center right*, races for the ball during a 1968 Eredivisie match. Since 2003, an award named after Cruyff has been given to top players in the Eredivisie.

Members of PSV Eindhoven celebrate after winning their twenty-fifth Eredivisie championship in 2024. The team beat Sparta Rotterdam 4–2 to claim the title.

made names for themselves in the Eredivisie. The league has developed a reputation for helping talented young players emerge as stars.

Three clubs have won the majority of Eredivisie titles. All but six championships have gone to one of the so-called "Big Three" teams. Ajax, based in the capital city of Amsterdam, has won the most national titles with 36. As of 2023–24, PSV Eindhoven has won 25 titles and Feyenoord has claimed 16.

EREDIVISIE FAST FACTS

First season: 1956–57

First champion: Ajax

Most titles: 36, Ajax

Most goals, season: 43, Coen Dillen, PSV Eindhoven (1956–57)

Most goals, career: 311, Willy van der Kuijlen

* Statistics through 2024

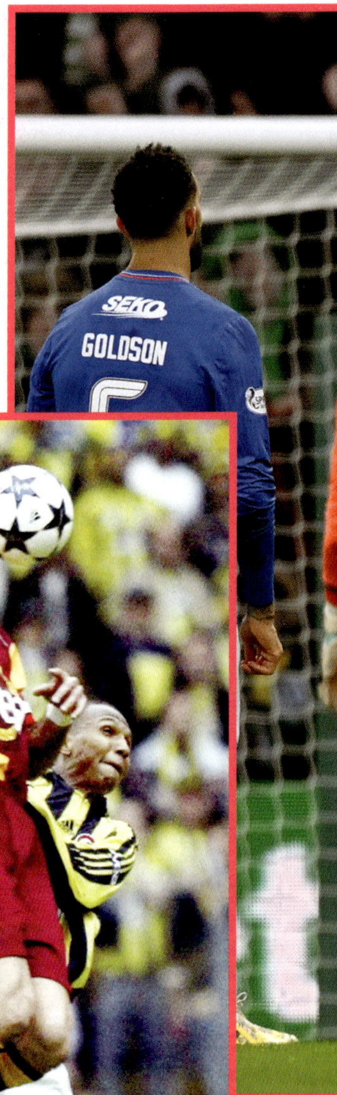

OTHER EUROPEAN MEN'S LEAGUES

While the top European leagues get much of the attention, other soccer leagues have flourished throughout the continent. The Turkish Süper Lig is led by three teams, all of which are located in Istanbul. Galatasaray has been the most successful team, claiming 24 titles through 2024. Fenerbahçe and Beşiktaş follow with 19 and 16 championships, respectively. Hakan Şükür, who starred for Galatasaray in the 1990s, is the league's all-time leading scorer with 249 goals.

Galatasaray's Hakan Şükür, *front*, hits a header during a 2005 Turkish Süper Lig match. During his 13 seasons with the team, Şükür helped it win eight Süper Lig titles.

Portugal's Primeira Liga has thrilled fans since 1934. Top clubs in the Primeira Liga include Benfica, Porto, and Sporting CP. Through 2023, no team had won more than Benfica's 38 titles. Besides the

The Rangers, *blue*, and Celtic, *white and green*, face off during a 2023 Scottish Premiership match. The rivalry between the two teams is known as the "Old Firm".

"Big Three" teams, only Belenenses and Boavista have won Primeira Liga championships. Star players in the Primeira Liga have included Eusébio, Ángel Di María, and Fernando Peyroteo. Peyroteo holds the league record for most goals with 332.

Scotland's top league dates back to 1890. Its latest name is the Scottish Premiership. The rivalry between Glasgow clubs Celtic and Rangers is one of the most heated in the world.

PRIMERA DIVISIÓN

Diego Maradona joined Boca Juniors in 1981. That year, he helped the team win a Primera División title.

Argentina's Primera División has been a men's professional league since 1931. But the country's soccer roots date back to the late 1800s. In 1891, Argentina became the first country outside the United Kingdom to form a soccer league. Over the years, Boca Juniors and River Plate have emerged as the most successful teams in the Primera División. The Buenos Aires neighbors have also become two of the sport's most intense rivals.

Argentina has won three men's World Cups. Countless world-class players have come out of the country. Though many eventually leave to join clubs in more competitive European leagues, these players usually get their start at home.

For example, Diego Maradona made his debut for Argentinos Juniors shortly before he turned 16. He scored

116 goals in five seasons. Later, he joined Boca Juniors for one season. Maradona helped the club win the league title and led the league with 28 goals. He then signed with Spanish giant FC Barcelona.

PRIMERA DIVISIÓN FAST FACTS

First season: 1931

First champion: Boca Juniors

Most titles: 16, River Plate

Most goals, season: 43, Bernabé Ferreyra, Tigre (1932)

Most goals, career: 295, Arsenio Erico

* Statistics through 2023

Members of River Plate pose for a photo before a 2013 Primera División match against Colón de Santa Fe. The match took place at Monumental Stadium in Buenos Aires, Argentina.

SÉRIE A (BRAZIL)

The history of men's club soccer in Brazil is unique. As far back as the early 1900s, clubs formed throughout the country. But the country's large size made it difficult for clubs from different parts of the country to play against each other. Because of this, Brazil didn't have a true national soccer championship until 1959, when the Taça Brasil championship was created.

Pelé was photographed wearing his Santos FC uniform and a wreath in 1969. The soccer legend is credited with helping Santos grow into a successful Série A team.

One top Série A club is Palmeiras, which holds the most titles with 12. Santos, which has won eight titles, is best known for its star player Pelé. Considered the greatest player of all time, Pelé began playing for Santos in 1956 at age 15.

He spent 18 years with the club, scoring

Members of Flamengo embrace after scoring a goal during a 2024 Série A match against Vasco da Gama. Flamengo's 6–1 victory moved the team to the top of the Série A standings.

569 goals in 583 appearances in all competitions. Pelé helped Santos win six league titles between 1961 and 1968. Flamengo, Corinthians, and São Paulo are other popular Brazilian teams.

SÉRIE A FAST FACTS

First season: 1959

First champion: Bahia

Most titles: 12, Palmeiras

Most goals, season: 34, Washington, Athletico Paranaense (2004)

Most goals, career: 190, Roberto Dinamite

* Statistics through 2023

In May 2024, the Central Coast Mariners became the A-League champion. The team defeated Melbourne Victory 3–1.

OTHER GLOBAL MEN'S LEAGUES

Top-flight men's soccer didn't catch on around the globe as quickly as it did in Europe. But the sport has had a rich history in many countries. The National Soccer League was Australia's top competition from 1977 to 2004. Then the A-League took over. It has been in operation ever since. The A-League crowns a regular-season champion and playoff champion. Sydney FC leads the way with five playoff titles and four regular-season championships in the A-League era.

Japan's top men's soccer league is called the J1 League. It was founded in 1992. The Kashima Antlers club has the most championship wins with eight.

The Confederation of African Football (CAF) sanctions leagues in every African country. The confederation dates back to 1957. It began with leagues in Algeria, Egypt, Ethiopia, Nigeria, and South Africa. Each member country has its own domestic league system. The top clubs in each country compete in the CAF Champions League and CAF Confederation Cup.

In the 2024 CAF Champions League final, Egyptian team Ah Ahly, *red*, faced off against Tunisian team Esperance, *blue*. Ah Ahly took home its twelfth CAF Champions League title.

WOMEN'S SUPER LEAGUE

The top competition in English women's soccer has existed since 2010. In 2011, the Women's Super League (WSL) replaced the FA Women's Premier League National Division as the country's top-tier league. It began with eight clubs. Many clubs were familiar to those who watched top-flight men's soccer. They included Arsenal, Chelsea, Everton, and Liverpool. By 2019–20, the Super League had grown to 12 teams, with dozens more playing in leagues lower on the soccer pyramid.

Manchester United's Ona Batlle, *left*, races past Manchester City's Yui Hasegawa, *right*, during a 2022 WSL match. The match ended in a tie.

Chelsea members Catarina Macario, Maika Hamano, and Niamh Charles, *left to right*, pose with the trophy after winning the 2024 WSL. The victory extended Chelsea's record number of titles.

In the 2018–19 season, clubs were required to form youth academies to train future soccer stars. This move brought women's clubs further in line with men's clubs. Arsenal won the first two championships. It won again in 2018–19.

However, fellow London team Chelsea has emerged as the league's most successful team. Chelsea was a founding member of the WSL in 2011. Between 2015 and 2024, the team claimed seven titles. Many top players from England's national team have starred in the league, including Bethany England, Ellen White, and Beth Mead. Australia's Sam Kerr won the league's Golden Boot in 2020–21 and 2021–22.

WOMEN'S SUPER LEAGUE FAST FACTS

First season: 2011

First champion: Arsenal

Most titles: 7, Chelsea

Most goals, season: 22, Vivianne Miedema (2018–19) and Rachel Daly (2022–23)

Most goals, career: 79, Vivianne Miedema

* Statistics through 2024

Barcelona Femení's Fridolina Rolfö, *center*, leaps into the air after scoring a goal in a 2023 Liga F match. The team defeated Real Madrid 1–0.

LIGA F

Liga F, the top women's league in Spain, has seen rapid growth in both talent and excitement. The league's history dates back to 1988. However, it has changed names and formats many times over the years. In the 2001–02 season, Liga F switched to its current format. Every season, each team plays the others twice to determine a champion. Beginning in the 2021–22 season, 16 teams competed in Liga F's top flight.

FC Barcelona Femení is Liga F's most successful club both domestically and in European competitions. In 2023, the club

LIGA F FAST FACTS

First season: 1988–89

First champion: Peña Barcilona

Most titles: 9, Barcelona

Most goals, season: 39, Verónica Boquete, Espanyol (2010–11)

Most goals, career: 442, Natalia Pablos

* Statistics through 2024

won its eighth title since 2012, giving it five more titles than the next-closest competitor. The team also reached the UEFA Champions League final for the third straight season. It beat the German club Wolfsburg in the final to secure a second championship.

Jenni Hermoso, the all-time leading scorer for Spain's national team, was Barcelona's biggest star for years. In 2018–19, Alexia Putellas became Barcelona's captain. Later that year, Putellas won the Ballon d'Or Féminin. This award is given to the world's top female player.

Alexia Putellas competes for Barcelona during a 2021 Liga F match. In 2024, Putellas announced plans to continue playing for the team through 2026.

OTHER EUROPEAN WOMEN'S LEAGUES

Other European countries also have strong women's professional leagues. Division 1 Féminine is the top-tier league in France. Like other European leagues, it features many of the same clubs as the men's league. The dominant club on the women's side is Olympique Lyonnais Féminin, commonly

Wendie Renard, *center*, lifts the trophy after Lyon's 2021 Division 1 Féminine victory. It was Lyon's seventeenth time winning the title.

SV Meppen's Vildan Kardesler, *left*, battles VfL Wolfsburg's Lotta Lorena Drews, *right*, during a 2024 Frauen-Bundesliga match.

called Lyon. With stars such as defender Wendie Renard, striker Ada Hegerberg, midfielder Eugénie Le Sommer, and goalie Sarah Bouhaddi, Lyon has won a record 14 straight league titles starting in the 2006–07 season. It also won a record five straight Champions League titles from 2016 to 2020.

In Germany, only two soccer clubs have claimed the Frauen-Bundesliga title from the 2012–13 to 2023–24 seasons. VfL Wolfsburg won seven championships in that span, while Bayern Munich won the other five. Before that, Eintracht Frankfurt and FFC Turbine Potsdam were among the league's top clubs. German teams won a record nine Champions League titles through 2023.

Members of Sydney FC pose for a photo before a 2024 A-League Women match. The team beat Melbourne City 1–0 to claim the title.

OTHER GLOBAL WOMEN'S LEAGUES

As women's soccer spread beyond Europe and the United States, competitive leagues sprang up throughout Asia, Oceania, and South America. The Australian national team reached the quarterfinals of the 2007 Women's World Cup. This led to the creation of an Australian top-flight league. Officials wanted to encourage the country's players to join home teams rather than look for competition in Europe. The first top-division Australian league formed the next year. In 2021, its name changed to A-League Women. Through 2023, Sydney FC had won the most titles with five.

Japan's top women's league is the WE League. This is short for Japan Women's Empowerment Professional

Football League. It began play in 2021–22, replacing the Nadeshiko League as the country's top competition.

Some of the most talented female players have come from Brazil. However, they gained recognition without having an elite professional league. Instead, most top Brazilians played professionally in Europe and the United States. The country is racing to catch up. Campeonato Brasileiro de Futebol Feminino Série A1, the women's version of Série A, formed in 2013.

Hana Takahashi, *left*, competes for the Urawa Reds during a 2022 WE League match. The team won the 2022–23 and 2023–24 WE Leagues.

DOMESTIC CUPS

In soccer, the league championship is a team's primary focus. Domestic cups give teams more opportunities to win trophies each year. These cups are open to teams outside the top division.

Domestic cups are usually single-elimination tournaments, which means the losing team is out. The competition plays out alongside the regular league schedule. The final takes place in spring at a neutral site.

England's FA Cup is the world's oldest domestic cup, dating to 1871–72. Any men's club in England or Wales can enter. This includes small amateur clubs and Premier League champions. Fans often support

Gary Lineker holds up the trophy after Tottenham Hotspur won the 1991 FA Cup. That year marked the 110th FA Cup tournament.

In 2024, Athletic Club defeated Mallorca to win its twenty-fourth Copa del Rey.

smaller clubs as they advance in the competition. The final is held at London's Wembley Stadium.

Some countries have multiple cup competitions. In 1960–61, England introduced a second men's domestic cup. The League Cup is open to clubs from the top four pyramid tiers. England also has a Women's FA Cup and an FA Women's League Cup.

Other countries have similar competitions. Spanish men's clubs play for the Copa del Rey. The Coppa Italia is held throughout Italy. Germany hosts the DFB-Pokal. In the United States, the US Open Cup is open to professional and amateur teams. All are important events on the world soccer calendar.

Members of Real Madrid pose for a photo before the first-ever UEFA Champions League final in 1955–56. The team beat Stade de Reims 4–3.

UEFA CHAMPIONS LEAGUE

The UEFA Champions League is considered the highest level of men's club soccer. The Champions League began as the European Cup in 1955–56. By that time, European clubs had been holding smaller tournaments among themselves for years. But as air travel and stadium lights became common, the ability to play weeknight games made a continental tournament possible. Sixteen European clubs participated in the first tournament. Real Madrid won the first five titles. Since then, no club has won more than three consecutive championships.

For its first 36 years, the European Cup was a single-elimination tournament. To qualify, a club had to win its domestic league. Those clubs were drawn at random to face each other in a two-legged series, with one match at each club's home stadium. The team with the most goals over those two matches advanced to the next round. The final was decided by a single game played at a predetermined host city.

1991–92 SEASON

The UEFA Champions League's format changed during 1991–92. The eight clubs that survived the first two rounds were placed into four-team groups. Each team in a group played its fellow members twice. The winners advanced to the final. This marked the first time the tournament had a group stage.

Manchester United's David Beckham, *left*, races past Bayern Munich's Samuel Kuffour, *right*, during the 1999 UEFA Champions League final. Manchester United defeated Bayern Munich in the famous match.

The 1992–93 tournament was the first played under the name UEFA Champions League. The competition's format has undergone many changes. For several years, its format was similar to the World Cup. Thirty-two teams began in groups of four. The top two from each group advanced to knockout rounds. This format created more games, which generated money through ticket sales and television contracts.

Beginning in 2024–25, a new "Swiss model" was introduced. Thirty-six teams begin in a league stage, each playing eight games. The top eight move directly to the knockout stage. The next 16 teams play a two-legged playoff, with winners moving to the knockout stage.

In 2024, Manchester City won its first UEFA Champions League title. The team defeated Inter Milan in the final.

Members of Real Madrid celebrate during a UEFA Champions League quarterfinal against Chelsea. Real Madrid defeated Chelsea to secure its place in the semifinals.

The Champions League is no longer limited to domestic league champions. Beginning in 1997–98, the runners-up of top European leagues could qualify. Today, the top four finishers in England, Spain, Germany, and Italy qualify for the group stage the next season. Other leagues also reserve spots for top finishers. Champions of the UEFA's remaining 55 member associations compete in qualifiers to earn spots in the Champions League field.

The Champions League is one of the world's most-watched sports tournaments. Some of Europe's most prestigious clubs have thrived in the competition. Dating back to 1955–56, Real Madrid has won 14 Champions League titles. Through 2022, AC Milan has secured seven championships, while Bayern Munich and Liverpool have won six each.

In 2021, FC Barcelona won the UEFA Women's Champions League final with a score of 4–0. It was the team's first time winning the title.

UEFA WOMEN'S CHAMPIONS LEAGUE

The UEFA Women's Cup began in 2001. It was renamed the UEFA Women's Champions League in 2009. Much like the men's tournament, the competition's format has changed over the years. Its name change in 2009 was accompanied by a new qualifying process. The top leagues were awarded two spots in the Champions League group stage, while the champions of the remaining member associations played to determine the rest of the field. This process has continued to evolve over the years. As of 2024, the bigger leagues are guaranteed up to three spots in the final 32.

French powerhouse Lyon has been the most dominant team in the Women's Champions League. Through 2023, Lyon had won eight championships. That included a five-year streak from 2016 to 2020. This matched Real Madrid's historic run at the start of the men's European Cup in the 1950s.

Three German clubs have won multiple Women's Champions League titles through 2023. FFC Frankfurt won four championships, while VfL Wolfsburg and FFC Turbine Potsdam won two each. Barcelona and Umeå of Sweden have also won two times.

Lyon's Amandine Henry races across the field during the 2022 UEFA Women's Champions League final. Lyon defeated Barcelona 3–1 to win the title.

OTHER CLUB COMPETITIONS

With so many teams worldwide, tournaments are also organized for those just below the elite level. Beginning in 1971, the UEFA Cup included the strongest men's clubs that didn't win their league championship. However, the field became less competitive as the Champions League opened its doors to more teams. In 2008, the competition changed its name to the UEFA Europa League. Teams eliminated from

Eden Hazard competes for Chelsea during a 2019 UEFA Europa League quarterfinal. Chelsea defeated Slavia Prague to advance to the semifinals.

In 2024, Grecian team Olympiacos FC defeated ACF Fiorentina to win the UEFA Conference League final. They were the first Greek team to win a European trophy.

the Champions League during qualifying rounds gained spots in the Europa League. The Europa League winner gets an automatic spot in the next Champions League.

The UEFA Conference League is one step below the Europa League. It formed in 2021–22, when the Europa League dropped from 48 to 32 teams at the group stage. The Conference League's field includes mostly clubs from UEFA's smallest leagues, along with midtable clubs from bigger leagues. The champion earns a spot in the next Europa League.

Teams from North America, Central America, and the Caribbean have their own club tournaments. The Leagues Cup involves teams from MLS, Liga MX, and Canada. It is a qualifier for the CONCACAF Champions Cup, whose field expands to the rest of the confederation.

FIFA CLUB WORLD CUP

Over the years, competitions pitted the world's top clubs against each other. The most notable was the Intercontinental Cup. From 1960 to 2004, it was an annual match between the European and South American champions. However, since FIFA did not organize such events, it did not recognize the winner as the world champion.

Eventually, FIFA created its own tournament. The first FIFA Club World Championship was held in Brazil in January 2000. Eight teams were invited, including two each from Europe and South America. The tournament also included one team each from Asia, Africa,

Karim Benzema holds the FIFA Club World Cup trophy at the Santiago Bernabéu Stadium in Madrid, Spain. In 2023, Benzema became the first to score in four Club World Cups.

CONTROVERSIAL COMPETITIONS

Because different playing styles were favored around the world, club competitions were sometimes considered uneven and controversial. Some South American clubs had a more physical, aggressive playing style that European clubs disdained. Several European clubs encouraged FIFA to step in and oversee an international club competition.

Oceania, and North America. Brazilian clubs Corinthians and Vasco de Gama faced off in the final. Corinthians won.

Financial problems put the tournament on pause for the next four years. But from 2005 to 2023, it was held annually. In 2006, it was renamed the FIFA Club World Cup. The field usually includes the champions of the six continents, plus another club from the host continent. The European and South American champions get byes into the semifinals.

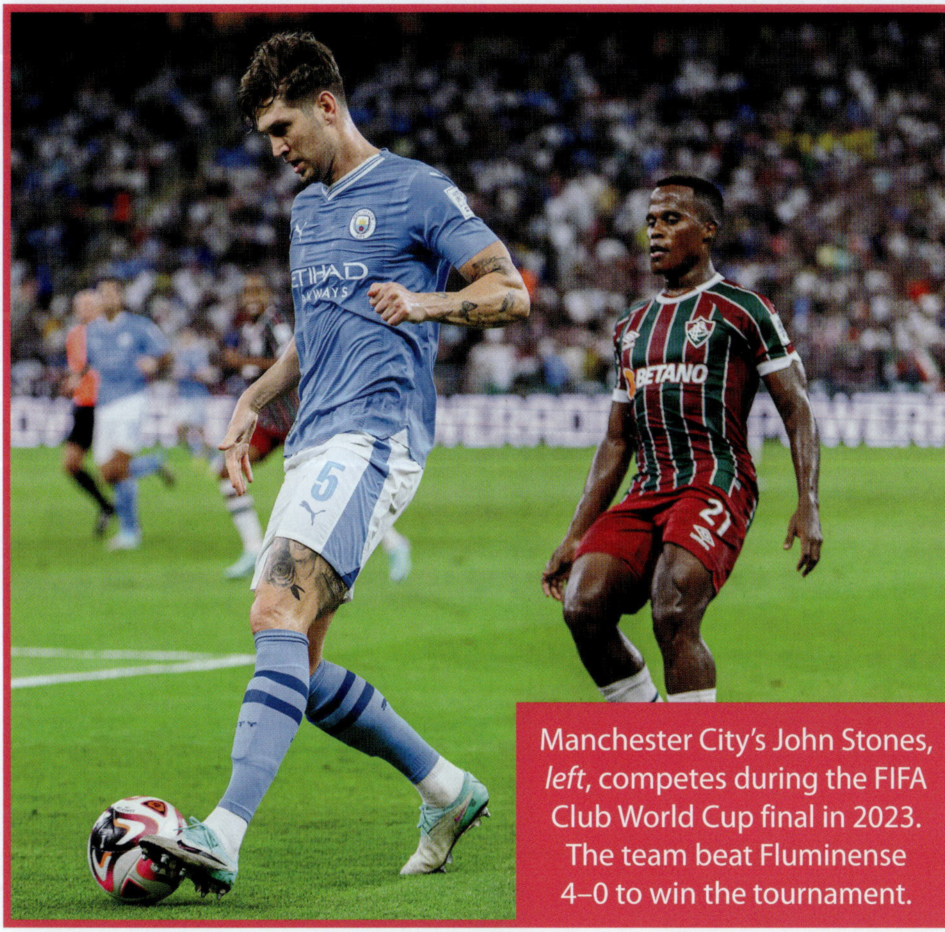

Manchester City's John Stones, *left*, competes during the FIFA Club World Cup final in 2023. The team beat Fluminense 4–0 to win the tournament.

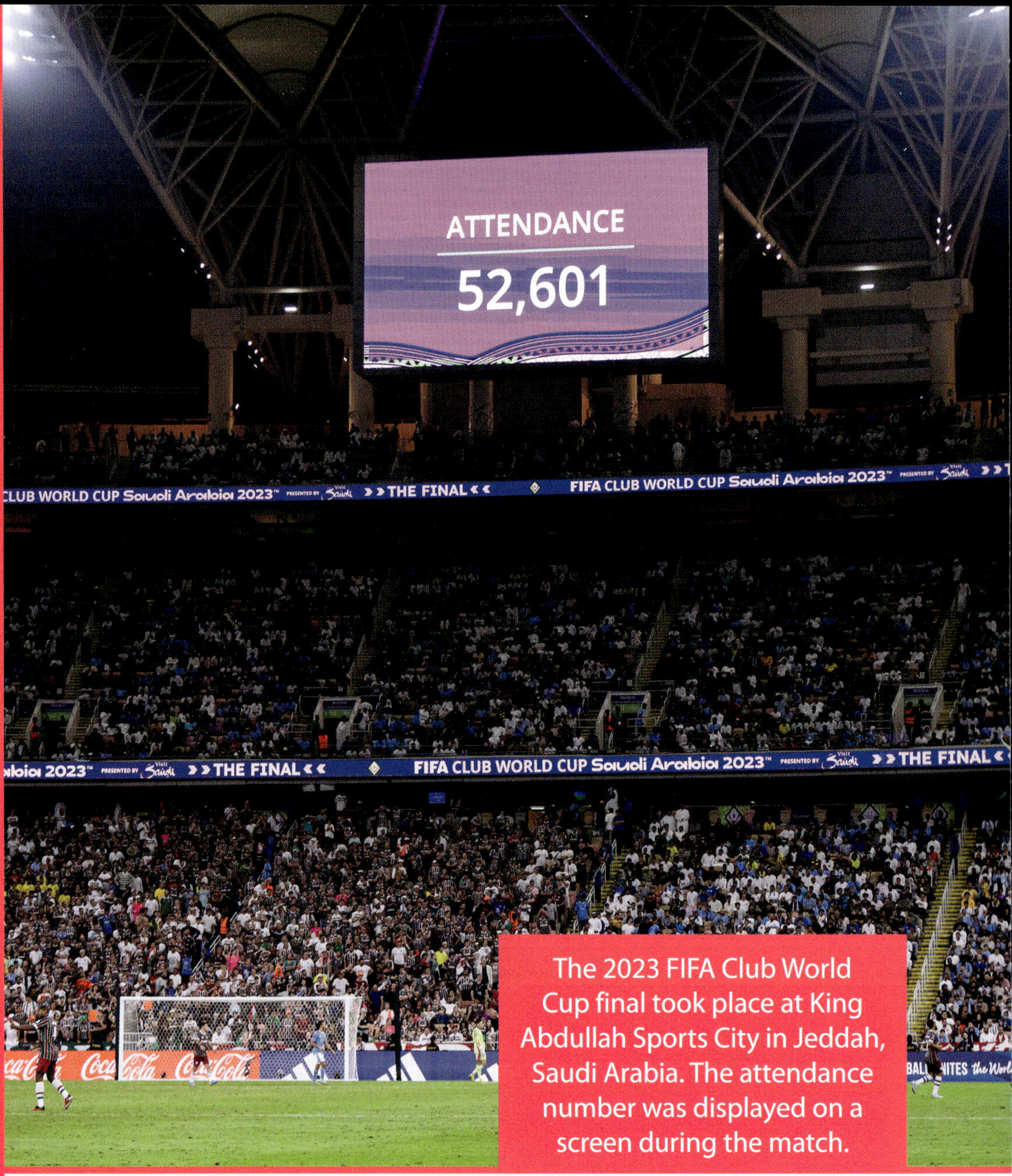

The 2023 FIFA Club World Cup final took place at King Abdullah Sports City in Jeddah, Saudi Arabia. The attendance number was displayed on a screen during the match.

The Club World Cup officially determined the world champion. However, the quality of the participating teams varied, and the tournament struggled to capture fans' attention. Because of this, the tournament didn't garner as much attention as the UEFA Champions League. Eager to change this, FIFA announced plans for an expanded, 32-team Club World Cup to begin in 2025.

As part of the changes, FIFA renamed the tournament Mundial de Clubes. The plan to expand the tournament was controversial, as many clubs objected to adding more games that would tax players' fitness and safety. But FIFA continued with its plans for a rebranded tournament. It was scheduled to take place in the United States in 2025. Under the new format, the Club World Cup will happen every four years. Eight groups of four teams will participate. The top two teams will advance to knockout stages.

In 2023, Fluminense's goalie Fábio became the oldest person to play in the FIFA Club World Cup final. He was 43 years old.

MICHELLE AKERS

A USWNT pioneer, Michelle Akers was the first women's soccer superstar. She was a member of the first USWNT to play in international competition in 1985. She also scored the first goal in USWNT history. It happened in a tie against Denmark on August 21, 1985.

Akers scored a team record of 39 goals in 26 games during the 1991 international season. During the first FIFA Women's World Cup in 1991, she scored ten goals to win the Golden Boot and led the US team to the championship. Akers later starred as defensive midfielder when the USWNT won again in 1999. She retired in 2000.

Michelle Akers was named FIFA Player of the Century in 2000. By the time of her retirement, she had logged 105 goals in 153 games.

NADINE ANGERER

Nadine Angerer spent nearly a decade as a backup goalkeeper on the German women's national team. When she finally got her chance to compete at the 2007 Women's World Cup, she made up for lost time. She did not allow a single goal in the net for 540 minutes of tournament play.

Through the 2023 World Cup, no other goalie has matched Angerer's six straight shutouts. Her skill helped Germany win its second consecutive Women's World Cup title. Angerer retired from pro soccer in 2015.

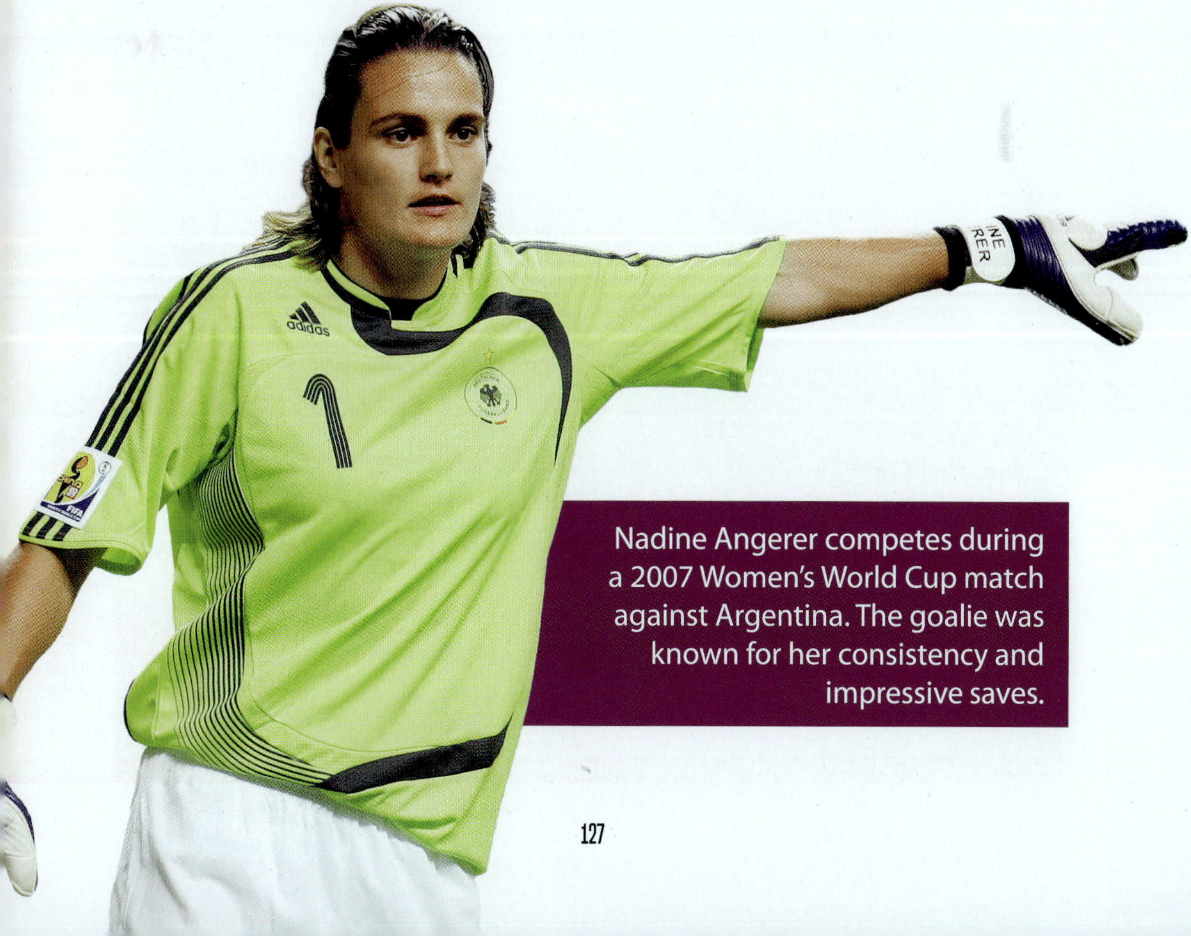

Nadine Angerer competes during a 2007 Women's World Cup match against Argentina. The goalie was known for her consistency and impressive saves.

ROBERTO BAGGIO

Roberto Baggio's creative play made him a star in Serie A and on Italy's 1990s national teams. Swift and sleek, Baggio was one of his generation's finest dribblers. He was also a set-piece specialist known for his graceful free kicks and goal-scoring skills.

In 2002, Baggio was named to the FIFA World Cup Dream Team. Fans voted on players they'd like to see on a team together. During Baggio's 16 years playing for Italy, he scored 27 goals in 56 international matches. This is tied for the fourth-most goals in team history. Baggio retired in 2004.

Roberto Baggio celebrates after scoring a goal during a 1994 World Cup semifinal. That year, Baggio became known for missing a penalty kick in the World Cup final, which cost Italy the title.

FRANCO BARESI

Franco Baresi is one of the all-time greatest defenders. He spent his entire 20-year career with AC Milan, commanding the team's defense as sweeper. Baresi made 710 appearances for the team, serving as captain for 15 seasons.

Baresi helped AC Milan win the UEFA European Cup/ Champions League in 1988–89, 1989–90, and 1993–94. He was also a substitute on Italy's 1982 World Cup–winning team. He later started for Italy in the 1990 and 1994 World Cups, helping the team finish third and second. Baresi retired after the 1996–97 season.

Franco Baresi competes for AC Milan during a 1992–93 Serie A match. The defender joined the club as a teen in 1978.

FRANZ BECKENBAUER

Franz Beckenbauer races across the field during the 1974 World Cup. The sweeper became captain of West Germany's national team in 1971.

Intelligent and graceful, German defender Franz Beckenbauer was nicknamed "Der Kaiser," or "The Emperor." He is credited with inventing the attacking sweeper position. He often sparked the offenses of his Bayern Munich and West German teams with daring runs out of his own defensive end deep into the opponent's half. Beckenbauer is the only defender to win the Ballon d'Or as the world's best player twice.

With Beckenbauer as captain, Bayern Munich won three consecutive European Cup championships between 1973 and 1976. Beckenbauer also captained West Germany during the 1972 European Championship and 1974 World Cup. The team won both events. Beckenbauer scored 57 goals in 535 games with Bayern Munich. In 1977, he joined the New York Cosmos of the North American Soccer League.

After retiring in 1983, Beckenbauer became manager of West Germany's national team in 1984. He led a reunified Germany to the World Cup championship in 1990. As of 2024, Beckenbauer is one of only three men to have won the tournament as both a player and manager.

Franz Beckenbauer competes for Bayern Munich during a 1977 Bundesliga match against Rot-Weiss Essen. Beckenbauer helped his team secure a 5–1 victory.

GEORGE BEST

Northern Irishman George Best was known for his flashy style during 11 seasons as a Manchester United winger. Best joined the Red Devils at age 15, making his first-team debut two years later in 1963. Right away, he set Manchester on fire with his talent and acrobatic play. He led the team to victory in 1964–65 and 1966–67.

Best also helped Manchester United win the European Cup in 1968. He scored 178 goals over 466 career games. Best died in 2005.

George Best, *right*, was famous for his fashionable style and skillful playing abilities. Pelé once called Best "the greatest player in the world."

Lucy Bronze celebrates after scoring a goal during a 2022 Women's Euro semifinal. Bronze helped the team defeat Sweden 4–0.

LUCY BRONZE

Known for her adaptability and attacking talent, Lucy Bronze joined the English women's national team in 2013 and played a key role in its surge to international prominence. With Bronze as an attacking fullback, England climbed the ranks to finish third in the 2015 Women's World Cup. Eight years later, the team finished in second place.

With a powerful and precise right foot, Bronze has starred with several top European teams. She was a main contributor for FC Barcelona's 2022–23 team, which won the Champions League title. Bronze was still playing in 2024.

GIANLUIGI BUFFON

Italian goalkeeper Gianluigi Buffon is regarded as the greatest of his generation. Nicknamed "Gigi," Buffon was a hulking presence in the Italian net during the 2000s. He started as goalkeeper for Parma in 1995. Standing more than six feet (1.8 m) tall, the Tuscany native also starred for the Italian team Juventus beginning in 2001. The club won ten Serie A titles with Buffon as keeper. As of 2024, he holds the record for most Serie A appearances with 657.

Buffon helped Italy win the 2006 World Cup title as well. Later, he played for Paris Saint-Germain and returned to Juventus and Parma. After a 28-year career, Buffon retired in 2023.

Gianluigi Buffon cheers for his Juventus teammates during a 2015 UEFA Champions League match against Real Madrid. Buffon and his team secured a 2–1 victory.

BOBBY CHARLTON

English forward Bobby Charlton was beloved by his countrymen. Just two years into his career with Manchester United, Charlton was one of 21 people to survive when the team's plane crashed in Munich in 1958. After the tragedy, he helped United return to greatness. Charlton scored 249 goals in 758 games, winning three league titles and one European Cup title.

Bobby Charlton competes during his final match with Manchester United in 1973. The team faced off against Chelsea at Stamford Bridge in London.

Charlton was also a force for England's national team, scoring 49 goals in 106 games. He was a starring member of the squad that won the country's last World Cup title in 1966. In 1994, he was knighted for his accomplishments by Queen Elizabeth II. Charlton died in 2023.

JOHAN CRUYFF

Few players have left a bigger mark on soccer than Dutch attacker Johan Cruyff. A smooth offensive machine, Cruyff helped make the Netherlands an international power. He embodied the Dutch philosophy of Total Football. Under this playing style, players have no fixed positions and can sub in for each other freely.

Johan Cruyff's soccer skills earned him the nickname "The Flying Dutchman." In the 1974 World Cup, his rebellious style and clever plays helped the Netherlands reach the final.

Cruyff dazzled over nine seasons with Ajax, scoring 193 goals in 245 matches from 1964 to 1973. He was an unstoppable force, winning the Ballon d'Or in 1971. He led his team to three consecutive European Cup titles from 1971 to 1973. Cruyff also dominated with the Netherlands national team, captaining the squad to a runner-up finish in the 1974 World Cup.

After a decade with Ajax, Cruyff joined FC Barcelona. He won back-to-back Ballon d'Or awards in 1973 and 1974, scoring 48 goals in 143 games. After retiring in 1984, Cruyff managed both Ajax and Barcelona. Cruyff's influence can still be seen in the playing styles of modern soccer. He died in 2016.

Johan Cruyff takes a shot during the 1974 World Cup quarterfinal. Cruyff scored two goals in the match, helping his team defeat Argentina 4–0.

ALFREDO DI STÉFANO

Nicknamed the "Blond Arrow," Argentinian center forward Alfredo Di Stéfano wowed fans with his endurance and scoring abilities. After playing eight seasons in South America, Di Stéfano burst onto the world scene with Real Madrid in 1953. He scored 308 goals over 396 games, helping the team achieve both league and European dominance for more than a decade.

Di Stéfano won the Ballon d'Or in 1957 and 1959. He spent 11 seasons with Real Madrid. During that time he won eight La Liga championships and five European Cup titles.

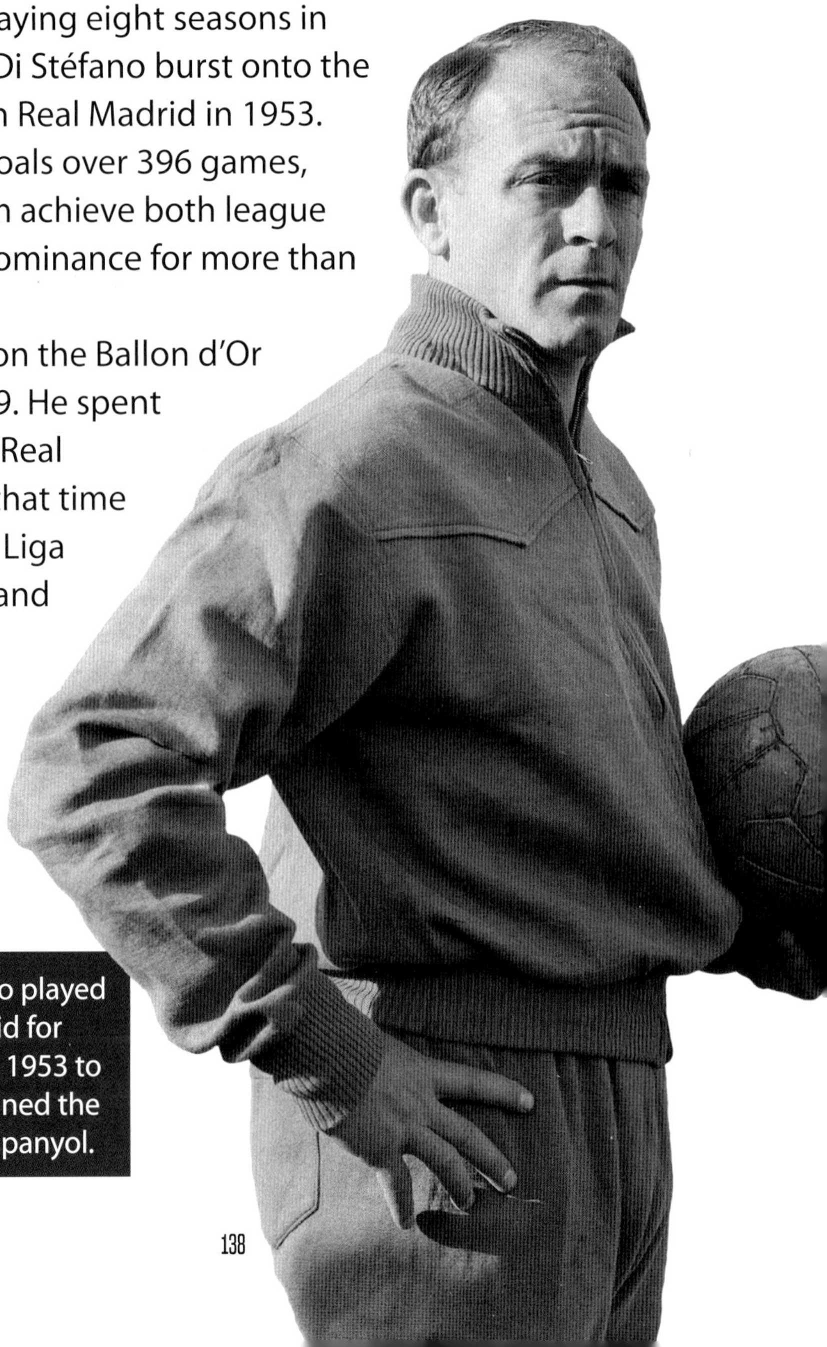

Alfredo Di Stéfano played for Real Madrid for 11 seasons, from 1953 to 1964. He later joined the Spanish team Espanyol.

Eusébio, *right*, competes during a 1966 World Cup group stage match. Portugal defeated Hungary 3–1.

EUSÉBIO

A fleet-footed Portuguese forward, Eusébio delighted fans with his passion and scoring touch at both professional and international levels. Eusébio was an unstoppable force for Portuguese team Benfica. The 1965 Ballon d'Or winner scored 727 goals in 715 games from 1961 to 1975.

He helped the team win 11 league titles and the 1962 European Cup. Eusébio also played with Portugal's national team for 12 years. He helped the team place third in the 1966 World Cup.

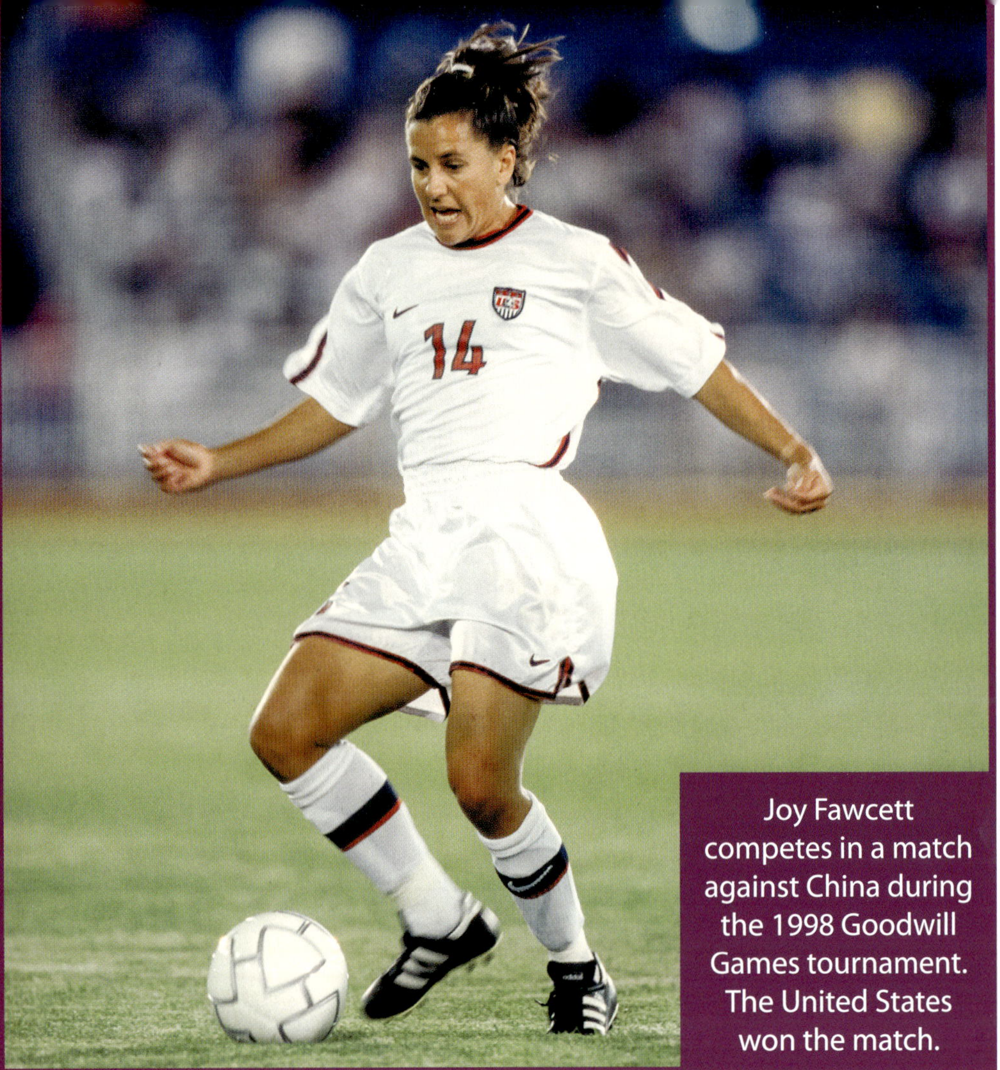

Joy Fawcett competes in a match against China during the 1998 Goodwill Games tournament. The United States won the match.

JOY FAWCETT

US defender Joy Fawcett was among the first women to wear the USWNT uniform. She was known for her persistence and scoring touch. Fawcett joined the team in 1987, two years after it started. She played in 239 games with the USWNT.

Over four Women's World Cups and three Olympic Games, Fawcett started 39 out of 40 games. She helped her team win two World Cups and two Olympic gold medals. In 2004, Fawcett retired as the team's top-scoring defender with 27 goals.

FORMIGA

Miraildes Maciel Mota, known as Formiga, was a star midfielder for Brazil's national team from 1995 to 2021. She was born in 1978, three years before Brazil overturned a law that banned women from playing soccer. Formiga quickly became a superstar. She played her first international game at age 17 in the 1995 World Cup. She is the only player to compete in seven World Cups.

Formiga's rock-steady midfield presence helped Brazil win two Olympic silver medals in 2004 and 2008. She also helped the team achieve second and third place in the 1999 and 2007 Women's World Cups. Formiga retired in 2021 at age 43.

Formiga competes in a match against China during the 2020 Olympic Games. It marked the soccer star's seventh time competing for Brazil in the Olympics.

GARRINCHA

Brazilian star Manoel Francisco dos Santos, known as Garrincha, was considered the greatest right winger in history. His nickname means "little bird," referring to how his legs looked after being misshapen due to polio. He played alongside Pelé on the Brazilian national teams of the 1950s and 1960s.

Garrincha was a skilled dribbler, helping his team win World Cups in 1958 and 1962. Garrincha won the Golden Ball as the top player of the 1962 World Cup, leading Brazil to victory. He died in 1983.

Garrincha, *left*, hits the ball past English defender Ray Wilson, *right*, during a 1962 World Cup quarterfinal. Garrincha helped Brazil defeat England 3–1.

ERLING HAALAND

Norwegian striker Erling Haaland grabbed the world's attention in 2020 with his scoring talent, speed, and Zen-like celebrations. After scoring a goal, he would sit cross-legged on the ground and meditate. After making his way through the Norwegian and Austrian leagues, 19-year-old Haaland signed with German team Borussia Dortmund in 2019.

Erling Haaland celebrates after scoring a goal in a 2022 Premier League match against Brighton and Hove Albion. Haaland scored two goals, helping Manchester City win 3–1.

Scoring nearly one goal per game, Haaland logged 86 goals in 89 games for Dortmund. He later crossed over to the English Premier League with Manchester City. Haaland has continued to be one of the most feared strikers. He logged 52 goals in 53 games during his first season with the team in 2022–23.

MIA HAMM

Mia Hamm was known for her goal-scoring talent and competitive nature. During her professional career, she competed with the USWNT 276 times.

When Mia Hamm was a teenager, the USWNT was in its early years. Soccer was just starting to catch on with young women. In 1987, 15-year-old Hamm became the youngest player to make the national team roster.

Hamm went on to star for the University of North Carolina, leading the Tar Heels to four college championships. She also made a name for herself on the international stage. In 1991, 19-year-old Hamm scored two goals, helping the United States win its first Women's World Cup title. She played in three more Women's World Cups, leading her team to victory in 1999. She also competed in three Olympic Games, winning two gold medals and one silver medal.

Hamm was one of the first female athletes to break into the national spotlight, getting endorsement deals and appearing in magazines and commercials. She was a fast, agile, and persistent athlete who could split defenses with her dribbling or fly past defenders to reach open spaces. Her scoring touch set Hamm apart. In 2004, she retired with a record 158 international goals. This record stood until Abby Wambach broke it nine years later.

Mia Hamm cheers during the 1999 Women's World Cup final against China. She and her USWNT teammates became known as the 99ers after winning the tournament.

SAM KERR

Sam Kerr has helped make Australia a force in women's soccer. She debuted for Australia's national team in 2009 at age 15. A powerful striker who is hard to catch, Kerr netted 69 goals in 128 games through 2023. She helped the Matildas become Women's World Cup semifinalists in 2023.

Professionally, Kerr is a leading scorer in NWSL and FA Women's Super League and has won three consecutive Golden Boots. Starting in 2020, she scored 58 goals in 75 games with Chelsea of the English Women's Super League. In 2024, she was still playing.

Sam Kerr is known for hitting headers and celebrating goals by doing backflips on the field.

Carli Lloyd smiles after scoring a goal in the 2015 Women's World Cup final. Lloyd scored three of the USWNT's five goals during the match.

CARLI LLOYD

As a child, Carli Lloyd defied her parents' wishes for her to pursue ballet. She preferred soccer instead. For 16 years, Lloyd was a dominant force for the USWNT. Known for her competitiveness and ability to step up, the speedy and shifty midfield playmaker became a US legend.

Lloyd debuted for the USWNT in 2005. She went on to score 134 goals in 316 games. She also helped her team win two Women's World Cups and two Olympic gold medals. One memorable moment happened during the 2015 World Cup final, when Lloyd scored three goals against Japan in the first 16 minutes, leading her team to victory. Lloyd retired in 2021.

During his career, Paolo Maldini, *center*, played in 647 Serie A matches. He scored a total of 29 goals in those matches.

PAOLO MALDINI

A determined and highly developed defender, Paolo Maldini was a keystone of the AC Milan back line. The Italian debuted for Milan at age 16, playing more than 900 games from 1985 to 2009. Maldini won 26 total trophies with AC Milan, including seven league championships and five European Cup/ Champions League titles.

Maldini remained a lethal defender in his final seasons. He earned the 2004 Serie A Defender of the Year Award at age 36. In 2007, 39-year-old Maldini was named Best Defender at the UEFA Club Football Awards.

Maldini was known for his ability to read the game and make perfectly timed tackles. He was highly respected for playing fairly. The club retired Maldini's No. 3 shirt after he retired in 2009. This is a common way of honoring players who retire. In addition to serving as captain for AC Milan, Maldini also captained Italy's national team for many of his 126 appearances.

Paolo Maldini competes for AC Milan in the 2006–07 UEFA Champions League final. Milan beat Liverpool 2–1 to claim the title.

DIEGO MARADONA

Argentine Diego Maradona was the poster boy for the exciting era of 1980s soccer. Considered the greatest player of the 1980s, Maradona had a small stature of five feet, five inches (1.6 m). This gave him an advantage as he sliced and diced his way through the opposition.

Maradona was a multiskilled terror for opposing defenses. The attacking midfielder also played as second striker on Argentina's national team. He displayed a vision for playmaking, combined with passing, ball control, and dribbling skills. Never one to shy away from the spotlight, Maradona was the team's strategic and spiritual leader.

Nicknamed "The Golden Boy," Maradona helped Argentina win the 1986 World Cup

Diego Maradona joined his first soccer team at age eight. In 1976, he debuted with Argentina's national team at age 15, becoming the youngest player to ever join the team.

Diego Maradona holds up the trophy after Argentina won the 1986 World Cup final in Mexico City, Mexico.

championship. He scored two famous goals in a quarterfinal game against England. In the first, he appeared to hit the ball into the net with his head. Referees were not allowed to use video replays at the time, so the goal was accepted. But replays made it clear that Maradona had punched the ball with his fist. When asked about the play, Maradona cheekily said "the hand of God" guided it home. Four minutes later in the game, Maradona scored "the goal of the century" after dribbling past four defenders.

MARTA

Brazilian Marta is considered the greatest female soccer player. A six-time FIFA World Player of the Year, the feisty striker was known for her intense playing style. Marta joined Brazil's national team at age 16, playing in her first Women's World Cup in 2003. In 2007, her team finished as the runner-up, with Marta scoring seven goals in six games. She earned the Golden Ball as the top scorer.

Marta dominated during her next four Women's World Cups, becoming the first player, male or female, to score in five World Cups. Marta's dominance continued in the Olympic Games. She became the first player to score in five

Marta celebrates during a semifinal against Sweden in the 2016 Olympic Games. The soccer star has competed for Brazil in several Olympic Games, helping the team win silver medals in 2004, 2008, and 2024.

Olympic tournaments. Marta won silver medals in the 2004 and 2008 Olympics. With 119 goals at the time of her retirement in 2024, Marta is the top scorer in Brazilian soccer history. She capped off her career by competing in the 2024 Olympic Games in Paris, France, winning her third silver medal.

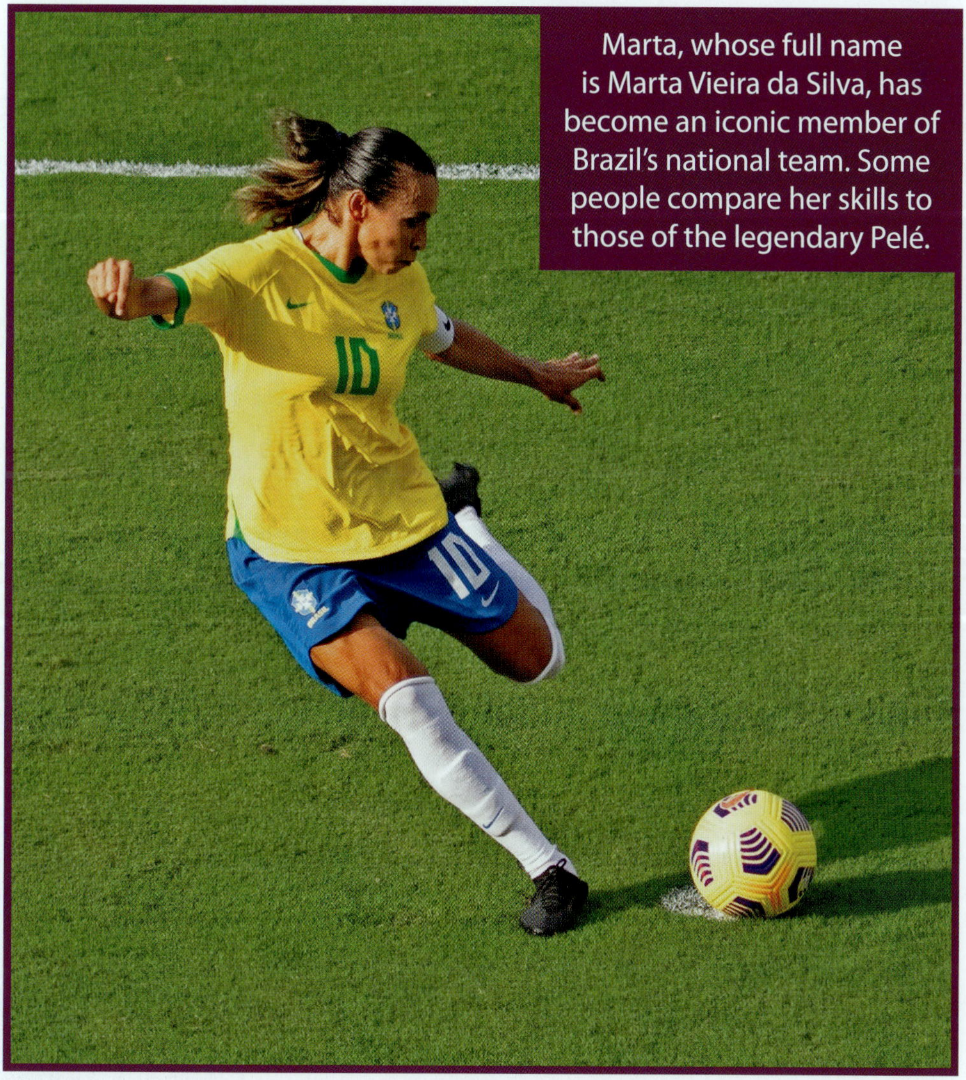

Marta, whose full name is Marta Vieira da Silva, has become an iconic member of Brazil's national team. Some people compare her skills to those of the legendary Pelé.

Kylian Mbappé takes a shot during the 2022 World Cup final against Argentina. Mbappé scored multiple goals during the match.

KYLIAN MBAPPÉ

Kylian Mbappé is staking his claim to be the greatest player in French soccer history. A forward with blazing speed, skillful passing abilities, and nimble dribbling talents, Mbappé had an impressive résumé by age 25. He debuted in 2015 with AS Monaco at age 16.

In 2017, Mbappé moved to Paris Saint-Germain, helping the team win three consecutive Ligue 1 titles. In 2018, the 19-year-old became the youngest French player to score in a World Cup. Mbappé scored four goals, including one in the final that helped France win. He was still competing as of 2024.

BETH MEAD

Forward Beth Mead has made important contributions to Arsenal and England's national team. With her slick passing skills and ability to create scoring chances, she has the most assists of all time in the English Women's Super League with 42. In 2015, 20-year-old Mead became the youngest WSL Golden Boot winner. Mead joined Arsenal in 2017.

Mead's talents helped England become an international powerhouse. In 2022, she was named Player of the Tournament as England won its first European Championship. That year, she won the Golden Boot. In November 2022, Mead took a break after suffering an ACL injury. In 2023, she was back on the field.

Beth Mead poses with the 2022 Player of the Tournament and Golden Boot awards after England's Women's Euro victory. Mead logged six goals and five assists during the tournament.

LIONEL MESSI

A record eight-time Ballon d'Or winner, Argentina's Lionel Messi is an intimidating player on the field. He is known for his strong scoring touch and ability to create plays for others. Messi has dominated the opposition at both the club and international level for two decades.

Since debuting for Argentina's national team in 2005, Messi has scored 106 international goals through 2023.

Lionel Messi holds up the trophy after Argentina won the 2021 Copa América final. The victory was Messi's first major international title.

Lionel Messi races across the field after scoring a goal in the 2022 World Cup final. Messi was awarded the Golden Ball as the tournament's best player.

This is the most goals by any South American player. Messi starred for FC Barcelona for 17 seasons. He won a club record of 35 trophies for the team, scoring 672 goals in 778 games.

In 2022, Messi earned his greatest achievement, guiding Argentina to the nation's first World Cup title since 1986. He scored two goals and again in a shoot-out to secure the team's victory over France in the final. In 2023, Messi took his talents to the United States, signing with Inter Miami of MLS.

Luka Modrić hits the ball during a 2023 UEFA Champions League quarterfinal against Manchester City. Modrić helped Real Madrid advance to the final.

LUKA MODRIĆ

A sturdy and persistent central midfielder, Luka Modrić was the beating heart of his club and national teams for more than 15 years. Many consider him the greatest Croatian soccer player. Modrić's precision passing from the inside or outside of his foot helped his teams find much success.

The 2018 Ballon d'Or winner has played a key role for Real Madrid, winning the Champions League five times as of 2024. He was also the driving force of Croatia's national team, which placed second and third in the 2018 and 2022 World Cups. As of 2024, Modrić was still playing.

ALEX MORGAN

Alex Morgan became the USWNT cocaptain in 2018, a position she still held in 2024. A swift and powerful striker, she ranks in the top ten in USWNT history in goals, assists, and multigoal games. Morgan helped lead the USWNT to Women's World Cup championships in 2015 and 2019. She also helped the team win an Olympic gold medal in 2012.

Morgan made her professional debut in 2011. In 2013, she played for the NWSL's Portland Thorns FC. Beginning in 2022, Morgan has played for San Diego Wave FC as captain. As of 2024, she was still competing.

Alex Morgan, *left*, won the NWSL's 2022 Golden Boot as the season's top scorer. She made 15 goals in 17 games.

GERD MÜLLER

Nicknamed "Der Bomber," or "The Bomber," Gerd Müller was known for his sledgehammer of a right foot. He averaged more than a goal a game for West Germany's national team. He scored 68 goals in 62 international games. In 1964, he signed with Bayern Munich, helping the team win several German Cups.

Müller was named European Footballer of the Year in 1970, becoming the first German to win the award. At the time of his death in 2021, Müller was twenty-first on the list of all-time international scorers. This was despite having played fewer games than every other player in the list's top 48.

Gerd Müller celebrates West Germany's victory in the 1974 World Cup final. Müller scored four goals during the tournament, including the game-winning goal.

Neymar, *center*, scored his seventy-seventh international goal during a 2022 World Cup quarterfinal against Croatia.

NEYMAR

Brazil has produced some of the world's most productive goal scorers. Neymar ranks among the nation's best. Through 2023, he had scored 436 goals in 708 games combined for club and country.

Using his slim frame to his advantage, Neymar combines quick reflexes, speed, and supreme confidence to terrify opposing defenses. During the 2016 Olympic Games, he helped Brazil win a gold medal. Neymar excelled with European teams Barcelona and Paris Saint-Germain before moving to the Saudi Arabian league in 2023.

In 1969, Pelé scored his thousandth goal while competing in a match at Maracanã Stadium in Rio de Janeiro, Brazil.

PELÉ

Generations of soccer fans consider Pelé the best player of all time. Elegant, graceful, and powerful, the Brazilian was a playmaking master. He seemed to read a defender's mind and could score with either foot.

Born in 1940 as Edson Arantes do Nascimento, Pelé joined Brazil's national team at age 16. He remains the only player to win three World

Cups, helping his country secure the title in 1958, 1962, and 1970. Pelé scored 77 goals in 92 international matches from 1957 through 1971.

Pelé is credited with popularizing the phrase "The Beautiful Game" to describe soccer. He played for more than 19 seasons with Brazilian powerhouse Santos, and the team often toured internationally because of Pelé's fame. After retiring from Santos in 1974, Pelé joined the New York Cosmos of the North American Soccer League. He helped fill stadiums in the fledgling league, increasing soccer's popularity in the United States. Pelé died in 2022.

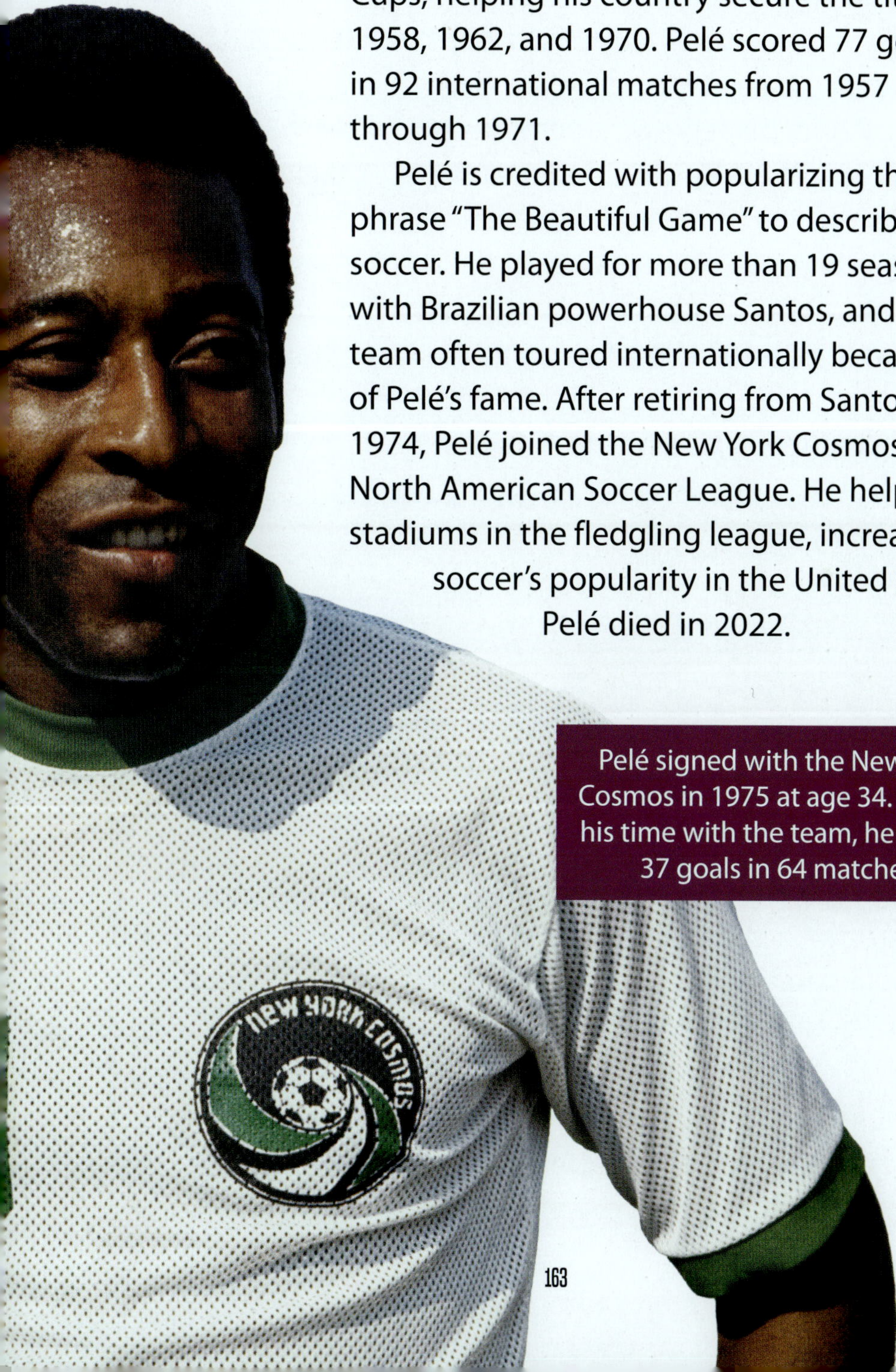

Pelé signed with the New York Cosmos in 1975 at age 34. During his time with the team, he scored 37 goals in 64 matches.

MICHEL PLATINI

His flowing hair dancing as he waltzed past defenders, Michel Platini was the face of French soccer in the 1980s. During matches, Platini displayed tremendous skill, creativity, and goal-scoring ability. He won three consecutive Ballon d'Or awards from 1983 to 1985.

Platini starred as an attacking midfielder for Les Bleus from 1976 to 1987, captaining France to the European Championship in 1984. Professionally, he was a standout player for the Italian team Juventus in the 1980s. He helped lead the team to a European Cup title in 1985.

Michel Platini played for several notable teams, including Saint-Étienne and Juventus. In 1976, he played his first match with France's national team.

During her career, Birgit Prinz competed for Germany in five World Cup finals, scoring 14 goals. She logged 128 total goals in 214 games for Germany.

BIRGIT PRINZ

Known as a superstar of German football, Birgit Prinz was a rugged and lethal striker from 1994 to 2011. She scored just 17 minutes into her debut for Germany's national team in July 1994. Prinz also became the youngest player to appear in a Women's World Cup final in 1995, although Germany lost to Norway.

Prinz returned to win the Women's World Cup for Germany in 2003 and 2007. She was named FIFA World Player of the Year three times during her career. Prinz retired in 2012.

Ferenc Puskás scored 83 goals in 84 games with Hungary's national team. As a member of Real Madrid, he logged 512 goals in 528 matches.

FERENC PUSKÁS

Regarded as soccer's first international superstar, Hungarian attacker Ferenc Puskás wowed defenders and audiences with his precise left foot. His scoring ability helped Hungary win a gold medal in the 1952 Olympic Games. Puskás also helped the team finish second at the 1954 World Cup.

After averaging more than a goal per game with Budapest Honvéd, Puskás joined Real Madrid in 1958. He continued to score at an astonishing pace, leading Madrid to European Cup titles in 1959, 1960, and 1966. In all, Puskás scored 802 goals over 792 games. He retired in 1967.

ALEXIA PUTELLAS

Midfielder Alexia Putellas is known as Spain's left-footed phenom. She has been a feared playmaker on both national and professional teams. Putellas has captained FC Barcelona to seven league titles and two Champions League titles.

A two-time Ballon d'Or winner, Putellas has been named UEFA Women's Player of the Year twice. She made her international debut with Barcelona in 2012. Later, Putellas helped Spain win its first Women's World Cup in 2023. In 2024, she competed in her national team's first-ever Olympic Games. The team placed fourth in the tournament.

Alexia Putellas competes for FC Barcelona during the 2022 UEFA Women's Champions League final. The team faced off against Lyon in the match.

MEGAN RAPINOE

Megan Rapinoe joined the US national team in 2006. She quickly became one of the sport's most recognizable faces and outspoken voices. She is famous for her creative, clever playing style.

A two-time Women's World Cup winner, Rapinoe scored 63 goals with 73 assists over 203 appearances on the national team. Her finest season was 2019, when she won the Ballon d'Or and FIFA Best Women's Player awards. In 2012, she helped her team win an Olympic gold medal. Professionally, Rapinoe has starred in both US and European leagues. She retired in 2023.

Megan Rapinoe made her professional debut with the Chicago Red Stars in 2009. Later, she joined Seattle Reign, scoring 52 goals in 121 matches.

Wendie Renard competes during a 2022 Women's Euro match against Italy. Renard and her French teammates defeated Italy 5–1.

WENDIE RENARD

Center back Wendie Renard has towered over the competition for years. She stands more than six feet (1.8 m) tall. She debuted with Lyon in 2006. In 2013, she became the team's captain.

Lyon is the most successful team in European women's soccer, having won 17 league titles and eight Champions League titles through 2024. For her efforts, Renard was voted to the Women's World Team of the Year seven times. In 2024, Renard competed in her third Olympic Games. Her team reached the quarterfinals but lost to Brazil.

During the 1970 World Cup, Rivelino scored three goals, helping Brazil reach the final. As part of the national team, he logged 26 goals in 92 matches.

RIVELINO

A patient attacking midfielder for Brazil's national team from 1965 to 1978, Roberto Rivelino was known for his long-range precision in both passing and scoring. He was commonly called Rivelino. His booming free kicks were the stuff of legend.

Rivelino is also credited with perfecting the "flip-flap" misdirection move, which has been used by many attacking players. The move involves a player tricking his opponent into thinking he is going to move in one direction and then moving in the opposite direction. Rivelino retired in 1981.

ROMÁRIO

Romário, one of Brazil's most beloved players, was known for his efforts on the national team from 1987 to 2005. Standing just five feet, six inches (1.7 m), Romário was a scoring master with the ability to direct the ball into the goal with the lightest of touches. The highlight of his career was winning the Golden Ball as Most Valuable Player of the 1994 World Cup.

Romário played in both South America and Europe. He was part of FC Barcelona's Champions League runner-up squad in 1994. In 2015, he began serving as a member of Brazil's senate.

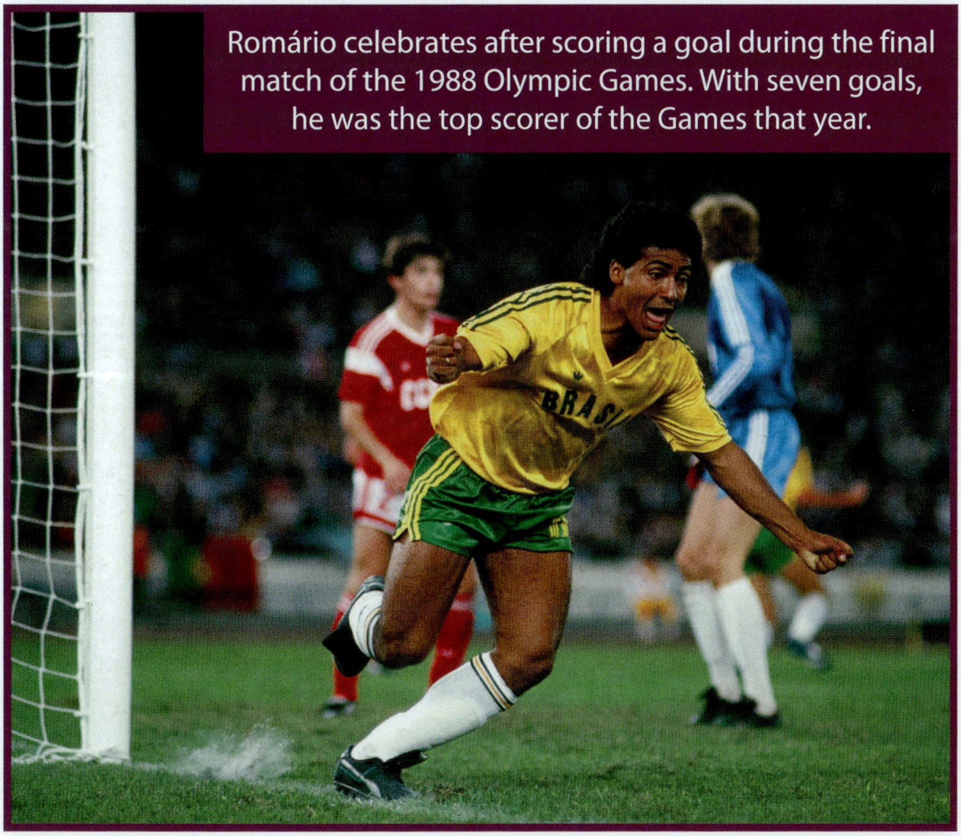

Romário celebrates after scoring a goal during the final match of the 1988 Olympic Games. With seven goals, he was the top scorer of the Games that year.

STAR PLAYERS

RONALDO

One of the most naturally gifted players of his generation, Ronaldo was the driving force of the Brazilian national teams in the 1990s and early 2000s. His unyielding pace and ball control drove Brazil to the top of international competition. After making the roster for Brazil's winning team at the 1994 World Cup, Ronaldo was a key figure in the team's runs to the 1998 and 2002 finals.

Ronaldo's dribbling and scoring abilities earned him the nickname "Il Fenomeno," which is Spanish for "The Phenomenon."

A two-time Ballon d'Or winner, Ronaldo earned the Golden Boot in 2002. He scored eight goals for Brazil during the World Cup. More than a decade later he remained the third-highest scorer in the history of Brazil's national team.

Unfortunately, knee injuries disrupted Ronaldo's seasons with European giants

Ronaldo cheers during a 2002 World Cup semifinal match. Brazil defeated Turkey 1–0 and went on to win the tournament.

FC Barcelona, Inter Milan, AC Milan, and Real Madrid. However, Ronaldo still scored 204 goals over 13 seasons. In 2004, he was named to the "FIFA 100" list of the greatest living soccer players. Ronaldo retired in 2011.

CRISTIANO RONALDO

An otherworldly talent whose fame skyrocketed, Cristiano Ronaldo was a five-time Ballon d'Or winner and three-time UEFA Men's Player of the Year. Through 2023, the Portuguese

Cristiano Ronaldo, *front*, celebrates after scoring a goal for Real Madrid during a 2012 Super Copa match. The team faced off against Barcelona.

player had won 33 trophies. These included seven league titles and five Champions League titles.

Ronaldo joined Portugal's national team in 2003 at age 18. He led the squad to titles in the European Championship and Nations League. But a World Cup championship escaped him. In 2022, though, Ronaldo became the first male player to score in five World Cups.

In 22 seasons playing for world-class teams, such as Manchester United, Real Madrid, and Juventus, Ronaldo scored 545 goals in 697 games. His success and smooth style have made him one of the best-known soccer personalities. In 2023, Ronaldo joined the Saudi Arabian team Al Nassr.

Cristiano Ronaldo holds the trophy after leading Portugal to victory in the 2019 Nations League final.

MOHAMED SALAH

With his scoring touch and infectious smile, Mohamed Salah is one of the most beloved players in Liverpool history. The Egyptian striker joined the team in 2017, scoring 210 goals through 2023–24. He helped Liverpool return to the top of the English Premier League in 2020, ending a 30-year league championship drought. That title came one season after Salah helped Liverpool secure its first Champions League title since 2005.

Salah also captained Egypt's national team. He was named African Footballer of the Year in 2017 and 2018. As of 2024, he was still playing for Liverpool.

Mohamed Salah, known as "Mo," has received three Golden Boots as the top scorer in the Premier League. He was the fourth player to win the award three times.

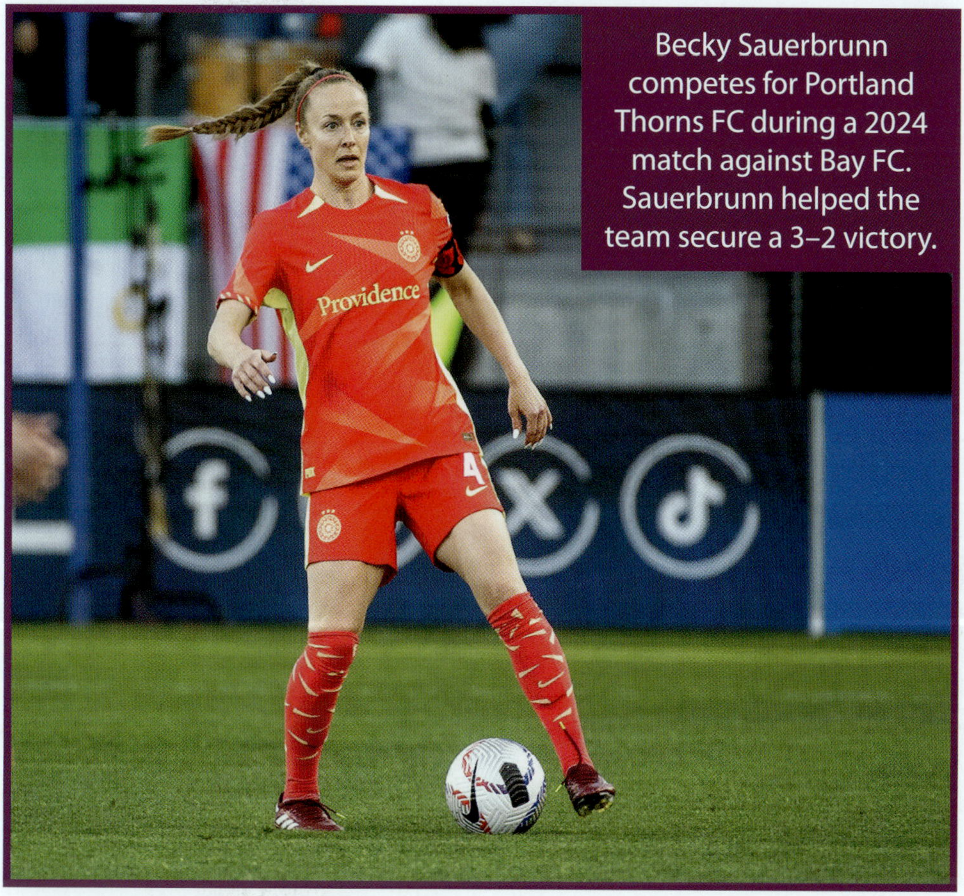

Becky Sauerbrunn competes for Portland Thorns FC during a 2024 match against Bay FC. Sauerbrunn helped the team secure a 3–2 victory.

BECKY SAUERBRUNN

Rugged and dependable, Becky Sauerbrunn became a vital contributor to the USWNT's back line after her 2008 debut. The center back's contributions helped the squad win two Women's World Cup titles and an Olympic gold medal. Sauerbrunn also showed her grit by playing every minute during the 2015 Women's World Cup.

Sauerbrunn was a key member of NWSL-winning teams in Kansas City and Portland. She also served as captain of the USWNT several times. As of 2024, she was playing for Portland Thorns FC.

HOMARE SAWA

Japan's Homare Sawa is considered the greatest Asian soccer player of all time. As the longtime captain of the Japanese national team, she led the squad to a stunning performance in the 2011 Women's World Cup. Sawa scored three goals in a group-stage match against Mexico.

The technically gifted midfielder scored a total of five goals to earn the Golden Ball that year. Japan, playing in its first major championship final, shocked the United States by winning the title in a shoot-out after Sawa scored a game-tying goal in extra time. In 2015, Sawa retired.

During the 2011 Women's World Cup final, Homare Sawa scored an important goal for Japan in the 117th minute of the game. Japan went on to win the match 3–1.

BRIANA SCURRY

Briana Scurry is known for playing as the US team's goalkeeper during the 1999 Women's World Cup, helping the team secure its victory. In the 1990s, Scurry was also the only Black player on the USWNT. Her stint as USWNT goalie lasted from 1994 to 2008.

During that time, the USWNT consistently ranked among the world's best teams. In addition to the 1999 World Cup title, Scurry was part of three third-place finishes in the tournament. She also won two gold medals and one silver medal during three Olympic tournaments.

Briana Scurry celebrates blocking a shot during the 1999 Women's World Cup final. Scurry's memorable save helped the USWNT win the match, inspiring many soccer fans.

CHRISTINE SINCLAIR

Striker Christine Sinclair is regarded as the most accomplished Canadian player of all time. She helped Canada become an international contender. She is also one of only three women to score in five Women's World Cups.

A powerful presence on the field, Sinclair debuted on Canada's national team in 2000. She went on to score 190 goals in 331 games, becoming international soccer's No. 1 all-time scorer. With Sinclair, Canada won two Olympic bronze medals and the 2020 Olympic gold medal. In 2023, Sinclair continued playing as forward for Portland Thorns FC. That year, she announced plans to retire.

Christine Sinclair kisses her medal after Canada's national team won the women's soccer final in the 2020 Olympic Games. It was the team's first time winning a gold medal.

ABBY WAMBACH

A hardened battle tank leading the attack, US striker Abby Wambach became the face of the USWNT. Her career lasted from 2001 to 2015. With 184 goals, she is the USWNT's top all-time scorer.

Wambach had a knack for scoring on diving headers. This put her at constant risk for injury. A diving header involves a player diving and using her head to direct the ball.

But Wambach was a key part of the USWNT's offense. She helped the squad win one Women's World Cup title and two Olympic gold medals. She was named FIFA Women's Player of the Year in 2012.

Abby Wambach holds up the US flag after the USWNT won the 2015 Women's World Cup final. It was Wambach's last time playing in the tournament before she retired.

GEORGE WEAH

Fleet-footed striker George Weah is considered one of the greatest African soccer players. He won the 1995 Ballon d'Or and was named African Player of the Century one year later. Weah was also a two-time league winner with AC Milan.

A multifunctional striker, Weah played the whole field rather than simply focusing on scoring. He retired in 2003. In 2018, he became the first African professional soccer player to become a head of state when he was elected president of his home country, Liberia.

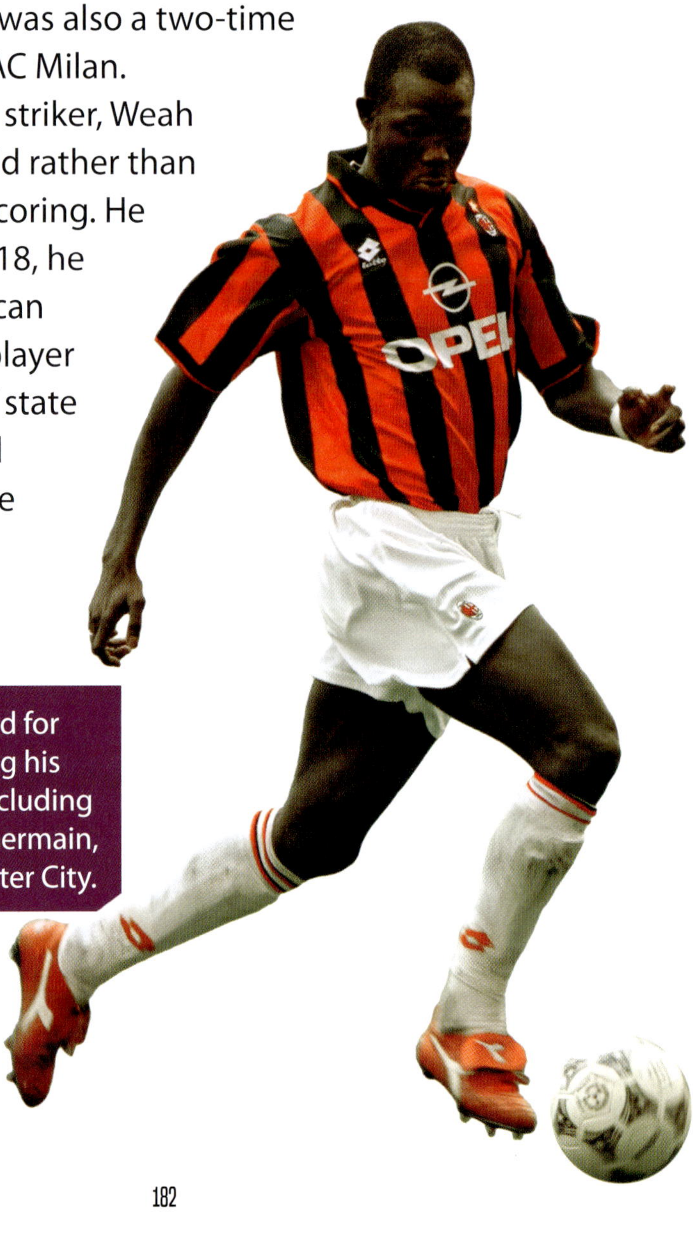

George Weah played for several teams during his professional career, including AC Milan, Paris Saint-Germain, Chelsea, and Manchester City.

Sun Wen played for China's national team in four Women's World Cups. At the 1999 World Cup, she received the Golden Ball and Golden Boot.

SUN WEN

The star of China's teams in the late 1990s, Sun Wen caused fear in her opponents from 1990 to 2006. Scoring 106 goals in 152 international games, Wen led China to new heights. After leading her team to a silver medal in the 1996 Olympic Games, Wen tore through the 1999 Women's World Cup field before China fell to the USWNT.

In 2000, Wen was named FIFA Female Player of the Century. She shared the honors with US player Michelle Akers. Wen retired after winning the AFC Women's Asian Cup in 2006.

Lev Yashin, *left*, dives for the ball during a 1966 World Cup semifinal against West Germany. The match marked the first time the Soviet Union had reached the semifinals.

LEV YASHIN

Goalie Lev Yashin was a major figure in Soviet soccer. Yashin originally joined the Moscow Dynamo sports club as a hockey player in 1945. He was soon discovered by the club's soccer goalkeeper, Alexei Khomich. Khomich trained 16-year-old Yashin as a soccer player.

Nicknamed "Black Spider" for his long limbs and black uniform, Yashin revolutionized the goalkeeper position. He was vocal in shouting orders at defenders. He also broke tradition by charging out from his goal box to take on attackers. Yashin became known during the 1958 World Cup. It was one of the first World Cups to be broadcast internationally.

Yashin logged more than 270 clean sheets with the Soviet Union's national team and with Moscow. His talents helped the Soviet Union win the gold medal at the 1956 Olympic Games.

He also helped the team win the 1960 European Championships. As of 2024, Yashin remains the only goalkeeper to win the Ballon d'Or. He won it in 1963. Yashin retired in 1970 and died in 1990.

In 1998, the International Federation of Football History and Statistics named Lev Yashin the best goalie of the twentieth century.

ZINEDINE ZIDANE

Zinedine Zidane was the face of French soccer for much of the 1990s and 2000s. He combined graceful elegance and technique with unyielding power. He played as an attacking midfielder for France's national team.

Zinedine Zidane, *right*, competes during the 1998 World Cup final. France defeated Brazil 3–0 to win its first-ever World Cup title.

Zinedine Zidane, *center*, was awarded the Golden Ball after the 2006 World Cup.

Zidane was named FIFA World Player of the Year in 1998, 2000, and 2003. He also won the 1998 Ballon d'Or. A renowned playmaker, Zidane scored twice during the 1998 World Cup final in Paris. France defeated Brazil in the match.

Zidane rose to prominence with French team Bordeaux. He gained fame with Juventus and Real Madrid. Zidane competed in Juventus's runner-up squads in the 1997 and 1998 Champions Leagues. He was also part of Madrid's Champions League–winning team in 2002. In 11 seasons, Zidane scored 67 goals with 57 assists over 339 games. In 108 appearances over 12 years, he logged 31 goals. After retiring in 2006, Zidane became a championship-winning coach.

GLOSSARY

amateur
A person who does something for enjoyment without getting paid.

bye
Automatic advancement to the next round of a tournament without competing.

clean sheet
In soccer, another term for a shutout, or when a team has kept its opponents from scoring.

confederation
A governing body of international soccer.

consecutive
Following one after the other, or back-to-back.

debut
To perform in public for the first time.

draw
A game that ends in a tie.

extra time
In soccer, two 15-minute periods added to a game if the score is tied at the end of regulation.

fullback
A defensive soccer player usually positioned toward the side of the field.

neutral site
A site for a match that isn't the home stadium of either team participating.

qualifier
A match that allows the winning team to advance to a tournament, or a team that has won a qualifying match.

sanction
To approve, organize, and agree to follow the rules and guidelines.

set piece
In soccer, a play such as a corner kick, free kick, or throw-in that puts the ball back into play after a stoppage.

shoot-out
When soccer teams take turns attempting penalty kicks to break a tie in a tournament game.

stoppage time
In soccer, the number of minutes tacked on to the end of a half for stoppages that occurred during play from injuries, free kicks, and goals.

sweeper
In soccer, a defender who plays the middle of the field and has the freedom to move about the defensive zone rather than stay with an attacker.

TO LEARN MORE

FURTHER READINGS

Hanlon, Luke. *The Best Matches of World Soccer*. Abdo, 2024.

Hornby, Hugh. *Soccer*. DK, 2023.

Marthaler, Jon. *The Best Teams of World Soccer*. Abdo, 2024.

ONLINE RESOURCES

Booklinks
NONFICTION NETWORK
FREE! ONLINE NONFICTION RESOURCES

To learn more about world soccer, please visit **abdobooklinks.com** or scan this QR code. These links are routinely monitored and updated to provide the most current information available.

INDEX

PHOTO CREDITS

Cover Photos: Matthias Hangst/Getty Images Sport/Getty Images, front (Kylian Mbappé); David Madison/Getty Images Sport/Getty Images, front (Mia Hamm); GDA/AP Images, front (Pelé); Alex Livesey/Getty Images Sport/Getty Images, front (Cristiano Ronaldo); Matthew Peters/Manchester United/Getty Images, front (David Beckham); Ira L. Black/Corbis/Getty Images Sports/Getty Images, front (Lionel Messi); Richard Heathcote/Getty Images Sport/Getty Images, front (Megan Rapinoe); Alex Caparros/UEFA/Getty Images, back (Aitana Bonmatí); Christian Ducasse/Gamma-Rapho/Getty Images, back (Diego Maradona)
Interior Photos: Paul White/AP Images, 1; Henri Szwarc/Abaca Press/Sipa USA/AP Images, 3; Michael Regan/FIFA/Getty Images, 4; Shutterstock Images, 5, 7, 16, 22, 56–57, 58, 78, 107, 122, 148, 168, 172, 175; Hulton Archive/Getty Images, 6; Popperfoto/Getty Images, 8, 10, 12, 36, 142; Bob Thomas/Popperfoto/Getty Images, 9, 11; Herbert Hoffmann/ullstein bild/Getty Images, 13; Wikimedia Commons, 14–15; The Picture Art Collection/Alamy, 15; Keystone/Hulton Archive/Getty Images, 17; Brazilian National Archives, 18; Intercontinentale/AFP/Getty Images, 19; Photo 12/Universal Images Group/Getty Images, 20; Fox Photos/Hulton Archive/Getty Images, 21, 32; David Cannon/Allsport/David Cannon Collection/Getty Images, 23, 41, 79; Alex Pantling/Getty Images Sport/Getty Images, 24–25; Wally Skalij/Los Angeles Times/Getty Images, 25; Kevork Djansezian/AP Images, 26, 52; Nick Tre. Smith/Icon Sportswire/Getty Images, 27; Michael Regan/Getty Images Sport/Getty Images, 28, 134; Pascal Guyot/AFP/Getty Images, 29; WCSCC/AP Images, 30, 38; Hulton Picture Library/Allsport/Hulton Archive/Getty Images, 31; AFP/Getty Images, 33, 40; ullstein bild Dtl./Getty Images, 34–35; dpa/picture alliance/Getty Images, 35; PA Images/Getty Images, 37, 184; Rolf Kosecki/picture-alliance/dpa/AP Images, 39; picture alliance/Getty Images, 42; Michel Lipchitz/AP Images, 43; Pedro Ugarte/AFP/Getty Images, 44; Jeff Mitchell/FIFA/Getty Images, 45; Matthias Hangst/Getty Images Sport/Getty Images, 46; Shaun Botterill/FIFA/Getty Images, 46–47; Tommy Cheng/AFP/AP Images, 48; Thomas Cheng/AFP/Getty Images, 49; John Buckle/EMPICS/PA Images/Getty Images, 50; Eric Risberg/AP Images, 51; Christof Koepsel/Bongarts/Getty Images, 53; Daniel Roland/AFP/Getty Images, 54; Kevin C. Cox/Getty Images Sport/Getty Images, 54–55; Maddie Meyer/FIFA/Getty Images, 57; Christian Charisius/dpa/picture alliance/Getty Images, 59; Bruna Prado/AP Images, 60; Fareed Kotb/Anadolu/Getty Images, 61; Rajanish Kakade/AP Images, 62; Kieran Galvin/DeFodi Images/Getty Images, 63; Jaime Lopez/Jam Media/Getty Images Sport/Getty Images, 64–65 (top); Raul Arboleda/AFP/Getty Images, 64–65 (bottom); Charlotte Wilson/Offside/Getty Images, 66; Rich von Biberstein/Icon Sportswire/Getty Images, 66–67; Simon Bruty/Allsport/Hulton Archive/Getty Images, 68, 112–113; Harry How/Getty Images Sport/Getty Images, 69, 70; Minas Panagiotakis/Getty Images Sport/Getty Images, 71; Victor Decolongon/Getty Images Sport/Getty Images, 72–73; Alan Schwartz/Cal Sport Media/AP Images, 73; Brett Carlsen/Getty Images Sport/Getty Images, 74; Rich Graessle/Icon Sportswire/Getty Images, 75; Leopoldo Smith/Getty Images Sport/Getty Images, 76; Ismael Rosas/Eyepix Group/LightRocket/Getty Images, 77; John Giles/PA Images/Getty Images, 80; Daniel Chesterton/Offside/Getty Images, 81; Terry Disney/Central Press/Hulton Archive/Getty Images, 82; Denis Doyle/Getty Images Sport/Getty Images, 83; Manuel Blondeau/AOP Press/Corbis Sport/Getty Images, 84; David Ramos/Getty Images Sport/Getty Images, 85, 117, 174–175; Elianton/Mondadori Portfolio/Getty Images, 86–87; Chris Brunskill/Fantasista/Getty Images Sport/Getty Images, 87, 176; Claudio Villa/Getty Images Sport/Getty Images, 88; Image Photo Agency/Getty Images Sport/Getty Images, 89; Anthony Bibard/FEP/Icon Sport/Getty Images, 90; Tnani Badreddine/DeFodi Images/Getty Images, 90–91; Guido Kirchner/picture-alliance/dpa/AP Images, 92; Markus Gilliar/GES Sportfoto/Getty Images Sport/Getty Images, 93; VI Images/Getty Images Sport/Getty Images, 94; ProShots/Icon Sport/Getty Images, 95; Musatafa Ozer/AFP/Getty Images, 96; Stu Forster/Getty Images Sport/Getty Images, 96–97; Michel Barrault/Onze/Icon Sport/Getty Images, 98; Gabriel Rossi/LatinContent WO/Getty Images, 99; Pictorial Parade/Archive Photos/Getty Images, 100; Wagner Meier/Getty Images Sport/Getty Images, 101; Luis Veniegra/SOPA Images/LightRocket/Getty Images, 102–103; Mohamed Elshahed/Anadolu/Getty Images, 103; Conor Molloy/News Images/Sipa USA/AP Images, 104; Harriet Lander/Chelsea FC/Getty Images, 105; Javier Borrego/Europa Press Sports/Getty Images, 106; Olivier Chassignole/AFP/Getty Images, 108; Michael Titgemeyer/Getty Images Sport/Getty Images, 109; Mark Avellino/Sportpix/Sipa USA/AP Images, 110; Hiroki Watanabe/Getty Images Sport/Getty Images, 111; Federico Titone/Anadolu/Getty Images, 113; Real Madrid/Getty Images, 114; Etsuo Hara/Getty Images Sport/Getty Images, 115, 124–125; Franck Fife/AFP/Getty Images, 116; David Lidstrom/Getty Images Sport/Getty Images, 118; ANP/Dutch Height/Gerrit from Cologne/Getty Images Sport/Getty Images, 119; Mike Hewitt/Getty Images Sport/Getty Images, 120; Nicolò Campo/LightRocket/Getty Images, 121; Marcio Machado/Eurasia Sport Images/Getty Images Sport/Getty Images, 123, 124; Rick Stewart/Allsport/Getty Images Sport/Getty Images, 126; Marcus Brandt/DDP/AFP/Getty Images, 126–127; Michael Probst/AP Images, 128; Alessandro Sabattini/Getty Images Sport/Getty Images, 129; Werek/picture-alliance/dpa/AP Images, 130; Werner Otto/ullstein bild/Getty Images, 131; Keystone/Hulton Archive/Getty Images Sport Classic/Getty Images, 132; Naomi Baker/Getty Images Sport/Getty Images, 133, 180–181; Don Morley/Allsport/Hulton Archive/Getty Images, 135; Roland Witschel/picture-alliance/dpa/AP Images, 136; STF/AFP/Getty Images, 137; Evening Standard/Hulton Archive/Getty Images, 138–139; Daily Mirror/Mirrorpix/Getty Images, 139; David Madison/Getty Images Sport/Getty Images, 140, 145, 179; Alex Livesey/FIFA/Getty Images, 141; Rui Viera/AP Images, 143; Mike Powell/Allsport/Getty Images Sport/Getty Images, 144; Matt King/Getty Images Sport/Getty Images, 146; Stuart Franklin/FIFA/Getty Images, 147; Christian Liewig/Corbis Sport/Getty Images, 149; Steve Powell/Allsport/Hulton Archive/Getty Images, 150; Carlo Fumagalli/WCSCC/AP Images, 151; Buda Mendes/Getty Images Sport/Getty Images, 152–153; Andrea Vilchez/Sports Press Photo/Sipa USA/AP Images, 153; Richard Heathcote/Getty Images Sport/Getty Images, 154; James Gill/Danehouse/Getty Images Sport/Getty Images, 155; Alexandre Schneider/Getty Images Sport/Getty Images, 156; Dan Mullan/Getty Images Sport/Getty Images, 156–157; Harry Langer/DeFodi Images/Getty Images, 158; Justin Fine/Cal Sport Media/ZUMA Press Wire/AP Images, 159; Karl Schnörrer/dpa/picture alliance/Getty Images, 160; Marvin Ibo Guengoer/GES Sportfoto/Getty Images Sport/Getty Images, 161; GDA/AP Images, 162; Bettmann/Getty Images, 162–163; Max Colin/Onze/Icon Sport/Getty Images, 164; Lars Baron/Bongarts/Getty Images, 165; Zentralbild/picture-alliance/dpa/AP Images, 166; Jonathan Moscrop/Getty Images Sport/Getty Images, 167; Thor Wegner/DeFodi Images/Getty Images, 169; Peter Robinson/EMPICS/PA Images/Getty Images, 170; Bob Thomas/Bob Thomas Sports Photography/Getty Images, 171; Markus Ulmer/picture-alliance/dpa/AP Images, 173; Lyndsay Radnedge/ISI Photos/Getty Images Sport/Getty Images, 177; Frank Augstein/AP Images, 178; Lars Baron/FIFA/Getty Images, 181; Professional Sport/Popperfoto/Getty Images, 182; Jeff Gross/Getty Images Sport/Getty Images, 183; Universal/Corbis/VCG/Sygma/Getty Images, 185; Oliver Berg/picture-alliance/dpa/AP Images, 186–187; Patrick Hertzog/AFP/Getty Images, 187

ABDOBOOKS.COM
Published by Abdo Reference, a division of ABDO, PO Box 398166, Minneapolis, Minnesota 55439.

Printed in China.
102024
012025

THIS BOOK CONTAINS RECYCLED MATERIALS

Editor: Laura Stickney
Series Designer: Colleen McLaren
Production Designer: Joshua Olson

LIBRARY OF CONGRESS CONTROL NUMBER: 2024938344

PUBLISHER'S CATALOGING-IN-PUBLICATION DATA

Names: Flynn, Brendan, author.
Title: The world soccer encyclopedia / by Brendan Flynn
Description: Minneapolis, Minnesota: Abdo Reference, 2025 | Series: Sports encyclopedias | Includes online resources and index.
Identifiers: ISBN 9781098296124 (lib. bdg.) | ISBN 9798384917120 (eBook)
Subjects: LCSH: Association football--Juvenile literature. | Professional sports--Juvenile literature. | Athletics--Juvenile literature. | Soccer--Juvenile literature. | Sports--History--Juvenile literature.
Classification: DDC 796.334--dc23